2.00

Bill Kyne of Bay Meadows

William P. Kyne.

Bill Kyne of Bay Meadows

The Man Who Brought Horse Racing
Back to California

Herb Phipps

South Brunswick and New York: A. S. Barnes and Company
London: Thomas Yoseloff Ltd

A. S. Barnes and Co., Inc.
Cranbury, New Jersey 08512

Thomas Yoseloff Ltd
Magdalen House
136–148 Tooley Street
London SE1 2TT, England

Library of Congress Cataloging in Publication Data

Phipps, Herb, 1906–
    Bill Kyne of Bay Meadows: the man who brought horse racing
back to California.

    Includes index.
    1. Kyne, Bill, 1887–1957. 2. Horse-racing—California
—Biography. 3. Horse-racing—California—History.
I. Title.
SF336.K95P48   1978   798.4′0092′4 [B]   78-60511
ISBN 0-498-02323-0

Acknowledgments

Thanks and grateful acknowledgments are extended to the following:

Gretchen Gunderson Kramer (librarian for the Kyne Library) for proposing that this book be written and assisting in the gathering of the data.

Robert S. Gunderson (president and general manager of Bay Meadows) for his encouragement and cooperation.

Nelle Kyne Morris (Bill Kyne's sister) for her cooperation and for contributing material.

William E. "Willie" Kyne (Bill's nephew) for the same cooperation received from Nelle.

Mae Feist De Vol (for many years Kyne's secretary) for her interest and assistance in assembling material.

Mel Patterson of the *San Francisco Examiner* staff for supplying much valuable data from the *Examiner* library.

Marylin Gunderson (Kyne's daughter) for her cooperation in providing material.

Prescott Sullivan and the *Examiner* for permission to reprint some of the excellent material he wrote about Bill Kyne.

Rusty Mathieson of the Bay Meadows office staff for typing the manuscript.

Thanks for information also are extended to Dr. William

5

J. Ward, Barry Whitehead, Mickey Dwyer, Jack Smith, Charlie Dougherty, Will Connolly and George Zarelli, Burl Tatum, R. E. (Lanny) Leighninger, Rusty Brundage, Ed Romero, Diane Nordoff, Les Vogel, Jr., June Pierce, Carl De Benedetti, Grace Gerken and Ralph Cunningham, Bob Wuerth, Vi Yazzolino, Bill Robertson, John O'Neill, Harold Hoertkorn, and T. J. Pendergast; to B. K. Beckwith for data in his books *Step and Go Together* and *The Story of Santa Anita*; and to photographers Doug Marchison and Frank and Steve De Vol.

Credit is also acknowledged for material from the files of the *San Francisco Chronicle*, *San Francisco Call-Bulletin*, *San Francisco Examiner*, and *San Mateo Times*, and for facts in the *Daily Racing Form* and the *American Racing Manual*.

Other sources were the San Mateo Public Library and the William P. Kyne Memorial Library.

Bill Kyne of Bay Meadows

1

When Bill Kyne was thirteen years old he was head altar
boy at St. Patrick's Church in San Francisco and his ambi-
tion was to become a priest. Then misfortune dealt him a
double blow. His father was killed in a ship-loading accident, and it became necessary for Bill to give up his plans
for the priesthood and get a job to help support the family.

His first job was selling newspapers for the old *Bulletin,*
and he took the ferry across the bay to sell papers at the
Emeryville Race Track. It was there on a summer afternoon
in 1900 that he saw his first horse race.

He was fascinated by the sleek, trim Thoroughbreds and
by the jockeys in their brightly colored silk blouses, but
he was even more impressed by the excitement and cheering
crowd as the horses broke from the barrier and raced for
the finish line. He watched wide-eyed as bets were made
and winners collected their money. Never before had he
seen so much money—and some of the bills were worth a
hundred dollars! It was then that the former future priest
became a future leader in the sport of horse racing, for at
that moment Bill Kyne knew his future was in racing.

It would seem logical that the youth's thoughts at this
point would have pictured himself as a jockey, a trainer, or

owner of a racing stable. But instead Kyne envisioned himself as the head of his own racetrack. And from that day on he never lost sight of his goal.

But if Bill Kyne had then known of the many obstacles, the disheartening setbacks and misfortunes that lay in his path, then one might wonder if he would still have chosen such a career. But judging from a close association of many years with Kyne, I am quite certain he would have. He was not a man that was easily discouraged.

He was not discouraged by friends who told him he had no chance of success when he announced in 1932 that he planned to get a bill on the ballot to legalize pari-mutuel wagering on horse racing in California, and to finance a campaign for its passage.

"Bill, the odds are 100 to 1 against you," advised a friend.

But long odds had never been known to faze Bill Kyne if he believed he was right. He smiled as he recalled backing another 100 to 1 shot—in the 1930 Travers Stakes at Saratoga. Among the entries was a horse named Jim Dandy, whose form was so bad he seemingly didn't belong in the race. But, as usual, Kyne had done his homework thoroughly, and in going back into the horse's past races he discovered in the previous year Jim Dandy had won a race on a muddy track by six lengths. The track at Saratoga that day was muddy, and he couldn't find a good mud race by any of the other contenders. Kyne made a substantial wager and Jim Dandy won easily, scoring one of the major upsets of the year.

William Patrick Kyne was born in San Francisco at Second and Clementine Streets in 1887. He was one of seven children born to John and Ellen Kyne, both natives of Ireland. The children were Rose, George, Jack, Grace (who died in infancy), Bill, Tom, and Nelle, who is the only surviving member of the family.

When John and Ellen arrived in this country it was at

10

the mines in Virginia City that John first found employment. Later they moved to Bodie, and it was there their first, Rose, was born. Shortly afterward, in the early 1880s, they moved to San Francisco, where John obtained a job on the waterfront. While working as a dock foreman in 1900, John Kyne was fatally injured.

In those days there was no workmen's compensation for accidental injury or death, and the Kyne family was left without funds and income. It then became necessary for the three oldest boys, George, Jack, and Bill, all teenagers, to find jobs.

Bill wasn't satisfied for long with his earnings as a news-boy and got an office job with Livingston Bros., a clothing store. "I hadn't been there long when I got fired," commented Kyne. "The lad working next to me pinched me on the rear and I started chasing him and my boss fired me."

His co-worker had acted only in fun, but Kyne had been reared in a tough "south of the slot" neighborhood where any aggressive action would result in instant retaliation. Self-defense was something a youth learned early.

Living next door to the Kynes were the Attells, whose son Abe became featherweight champion of the world; and down the block lived Willie Ritchie, later to whip Ad Walgast for the lightweight title. Another member of the neighborhood, Jimmy Britt, grew up to win two world titles.

Two of Bill Kyne's closest boyhood friends were Tom Maloney and Al Uniack. "When we were kids Bill and I earned spending money by collecting and selling scrap metal," said Maloney. "We were partners and split whatever we made." Maloney later became a state legislator and co-author of the horse-racing bill under which California tracks now operate. Uniack became the owner of a printing firm in Los Angeles and was one of Kyne's closest life-long friends.

But losing his job at Livingston's didn't keep Kyne idle for long. He got a better job with Bradstreet at twelve dollars a month.

"I worked in the office and delivered credit reports," said Kyne. One of the firms I delivered reports to was Sunfire Insurance, and the manager there offered me a job at fifteen dollars per month and I took it. I wrote policies and did some other work. After two years I was making fifty dollars a month; and that was pretty good for a boy my age in those days."

With a bright future in the insurance business seemingly assured, Kyne suddenly quit his job. It was racing that held his interest, and he went to work at the Emeryville track as clerk for Barney Schreiber, a prominent bookmaker. There he learned the bookmaking business, which was then legal. He also learned the knack of handicapping and pricemaking.

When the racing season closed, Kyne turned to business ventures on his own. He opened the Ironmen's Social Club, a recreation establishment with card and pool tables, and also began promoting boxing matches at the old Union Athletic Club. In 1910 he conducted a "white hope" contest, hoping to produce a challenger for the reigning black champion, Jack Johnson, but was unsuccessful.

After his venture as a fight promoter Kyne became involved in motion pictures as the manager of Bronco Billy Anderson, the first cowboy star of the movies, at Niles, California.

Hollywood had not yet become famous, and it was at Niles that the Essanay Studio was shooting many of the early motion pictures. Anderson, who gained fame for his role in *The Great Train Robbery*, starred in 150 movies filmed at Niles between 1910 and 1915.

Among other actors and actresses who appeared in Essanay films made at Niles and who rose to stardom were Wallace Beery, Ben Turpin, Marie Dressler, Jimmy Gleason, Zasu Pitts, and Ethel Clayton. It was also at Niles that

Charlie Chaplin starred in *The Tramp*.

Kyne and Wallace Beery became close friends, and when Bill opened his Bay Meadows Race Track in San Mateo in 1934, Beery came up from Hollywood as Kyne's guest, and he and Mrs. Kyne cut the ribbon, officially opening the plant.

Later Bill Kyne's sister Nelle had a chance to get into the movies at Hollywood. Nelle and Alma Ruben were schoolgirl chums, and when Alma became a star in Hollywood she invited Nelle to visit her. While Nelle, who was a pretty girl, was there, Alma got a part for her in a picture Alma was soon to make.

Bill Kyne's sister Nelle in her younger days—when Bill squelched her chance for a career in the movies.

"When Bill heard about it he put his foot down and said I couldn't take the part," said Nelle. "And he made me come home."

Since she didn't have a father, it was Bill who looked after his little sister, and he said he didn't want her "getting mixed up with that fast Hollywood bunch."

Alma Ruben later was reported in the press to have become addicted to drugs. She died of pneumonia at thirty-two.

Had Kyne stayed with Bronco Billy he might have wound up in Hollywood and a movie tycoon, but it was the lure of horse racing that again drew him back to the sport. Racing in California had been banned by a vote of the people in 1910, and the nearest racing was at Butte, Montana. Kyne went to Butte (then a prosperous mining town) in 1912 and went into business for himself as a bookmaker.

At twenty-five he was the youngest bookmaker in the country, and they called him the "boy bookie." And he was matching his wits against some of the sharpest men in the business—Ed Soule, Barney Schreiber, his former employer, George Rose, and Lawler Meehan.

But Bill devoted much time to studying charts and other factors in handicapping and became an astute pricemaker. He posted his own odds for others to bet on and made a pile of money. The copper mines were running three shifts, the miners were getting fat paychecks, and money was plentiful at the track.

One day there was a race in which the betting was heavy on two horses, John Graham and Christmas Eve. The other books listed them at short odds, but Bill had made Electric his favorite, and Electric was 10 to 1 on the other boards. The other bookies laid off most of their money on the two hot horses to Bill and he bet it back to them on Electric. Electric won and Bill cleaned up a small fortune.

Later Kyne bought and raced a large stable of his own, but not for long. He decided that was not his forte, and he sold the horses.

Then in 1915 came his first opportunity to participate in the ownership and operation of a racetrack. He invested $50,000 in a track to be built at Tijuana by James (Sunny Jim) Coffroth, a colorful and prominent boxing promoter. With both horse racing and boxing having been banned in

Bill Kyne in 1914 at the wheel of his first car (thought to be at Butte, Montana, racetrack). In the front seat is George Schilling, a racing official, and standing in back is Bill's brother, Tom.

California, Kyne and Coffroth had visions of the Mexican border town as a Mecca for sports fans and tourists.

Originally the track was to have opened on Labor Day, but construction delays caused numerous postponements, and it wasn't until January 1, 1916, that the Lower California Jockey Club's gala opening day of the one hundred-day meeting at Tijuana arrived.

Despite wet weather and a track ankle-deep in mud, a crowd of ten thousand was on hand, including Governor Esteban Cantu and a host of sports and motion-picture celebrities from the American side.

Kyne and other investors in the track were pleased with the opening, but five days later rain returned. As the rains continued day after day the weather became a grave concern. The track was located about a quarter mile down the road from the border gate and near the bank of the Tijuana River. A huge ditch had been dug between the river and the stands, and this was thought to be sufficient protection against overflow.

The storm in the Tijuana and San Diego areas developed into the worst on record. With water in the Tijuana River over its banks and threatening the stands and stables, the new racetrack closed on January 18, and all horses were evacuated. Then the Tijuana River went on a raging rampage, nearly a mile wide, and devastated the racing plant.

Eighteen days after it had opened the new track was out of business. Worse yet, the Lower California Jockey Club was broke, and so was Bill Kyne. He was then twenty-nine.

Losing $50,000 was a blow that hurt, but Kyne took it without flinching or brooding. Perhaps it was the basis for his philosophical expression that "In life you have to take the bitter as well as the sweet."

Kyne returned home and joined the Navy to serve in World War I.

Meanwhile, Coffroth raised new capital, rebuilt the Tijuana track, and it operated successfully until the new Agua Caliente track opened in 1930.

After his discharge Kyne returned home, and in the summer of 1920 he went to New York to try his skill as a bookmaker on the big time. (Bookmaking was legal on the New York tracks until replaced by the pari-mutuel system in 1939.)

Things went well the first few weeks, and then came the Dwyer Handicap at Aqueduct with the great Man o' War listed a 1 to 5 favorite. In fourteen starts the champion had lost only one race, in which he had stumbled at the start.

In the betting ring customers would try to wager on Man o' War and were told, "We're not booking him. Try that kid from the coast," and they would point to Kyne's betting stand. "Sure, I'm booking the horse," Kyne told

16

them. He started taking bets and never stopped until the barrier was sprung. Kyne had bet on Upset when the horse handed Man o' War his only defeat, and now he thought John P. Grier, carrying 108 pounds to 126 for Man o' War, would be the winner. If he was right he would win a hundred thousand dollars, but he was wrong. Man o' War won by a length and a half.

Soon Kyne discovered he had miscalculated and he ran out of money before all bets were paid off. "You'll get your money, just give me a few days," he told the others.

Bill wired his friend Lawler Meehan in Butte for $5,000. (Being a bookie, Meehan was accustomed to dealing only in cash.) A few days later Kyne was informed by Wells Fargo Express that a package had arrived. When he went to pick it up he was given a heavy potato sack. It contained 1,000 silver dollars and $4,000 in currency! And racetrackers coined a new word for money—potatoes.

Years later one of Bill's friends composed the following poem:

B I L L   K Y N E

❋

By Carl H. Koch

I knew a man; that is, I knew him when
He stood like Daniel in the lion's den
On Aqueduct's turf by the east coast shore
To meet all the wagers on Man o' War.

This west coast kid, called "The Kid from the Coast,"
Received a welcome and many a toast. . . .
Thanks, Lawler Meehan, for your potatoes
That saved Bill Kyne from some ripe tomatoes.

Shipped by Wells Fargo from Butte, Montana,
This spud sack with five grand made Bill a Santa

On that eastern turf in nineteen-twenty,
Where those silver dollars cooled off plenty.

Bill Kyne was a real friend with friends galore
Who could win or lose and venture some more.
Yes, Bill could draw water for any pool
Because he believed in The Golden Rule.

Soldier of Fortune, Adventurer, Friend,
Promoter, Builder, you were "A God-send,"
For the sermons you preached in your own kind way
In the annals of sports are here to stay.

Bill Kyne returned to San Francisco that fall and opened a restaurant on Ellis Street. "It was a good restaurant," said Bill, "but in time it went broke. I guess the cooks carried off too many hams."

But Solly Tichner, a friend from boyhood and later Kyne's program manager, had another version of why the restaurant went out of business. "It wasn't the cooks, it was Kyne and all the bums he was feeding. Any time a guy came in and said he was broke and hungry Kyne would see that he got a full meal, not just a skimpy handout," said Solly. "He got a reputation as an easy mark and was feeding nearly as many moochers as paying customers. His restaurant was the St. Anthony's Dining Room* of those days."

When informed of Solly's remarks Bill Kyne merely grinned.

According to his sister Nelle, Bill Kyne's compassion for the unfortunate and down-and-outer stemmed from his mother's teachings and examples. "Our mother never said 'no' to a person in need," said Nelle.

"One day a young man came to the door in ragged clothes and shoes that were coming apart. Before he could say anything Ma said, 'You poor soul, you're down on your

---

* A place in San Francisco where free meals are served.

luck, now you just wait right here.' She went up to Bill's room, got a pair of pants, a shirt and a tie, and a new pair of expensive shoes Bill had bought a few days before and gave them to the man. Then she handed him a five-dollar bill and said, 'Now you go get yourself a bath and a good meal and then you can look for a job.'"

Next morning Bill called down from his room, "Ma, where are my new shoes?" When his mother explained, Bill said, "But couldn't you have given him an old pair?"

"No, he needed the new ones more than you; you've got money in your pocket and you can go buy yourself some more."

In 1923 Kyne got back into racing, this time to stay. Obtaining financial backing, he formed the Silver State Jockey Club and opened a spring race meeting at Reno. The meeting finished with a deficit of $22,000. He went back in the fall for another meeting. This time it lost $12,000. When it was over Kyne commented, "Well, that proves fall is the best time to race in Reno."

He didn't try Reno again until 1931, the year gambling casinos were legalized in Nevada. With his friend Jack Dempsey as partner, Kyne staged a heavyweight boxing match at the track between Max Baer, who later gained the heavyweight title, and Paulino Uzcudun. The bout was fought under a broiling 4th of July sun, and Paulino won by a close decision. This meeting also was a loser, and Kyne scratched Reno.

Kyne had followed the second 1923 Reno meeting with a successful season the next year at Salt Lake City and raced there once or twice yearly through 1928. It was at the 1927 meeting that Johnny Longden rode his first winner.

Kyne conducted races at Phoenix in 1926–27–28–29, at Tulsa in 1927–28–29–30, at Juarez, Mexico, in the spring and fall of 1926, at Gresham, Oregon (near Portland), in

At Juarez in 1926. Bill Kyne is in white trousers and at his left is Jack Dempsey. Behind the two is "Sec" Morrison, racing secretary. The youth second from left in cap is Willie Kyne, Bill's nephew.

1930 and 1933, at Kansas City in 1929 through 1937.

At Phoenix one day Mickey Dwyer, a calculator at the track, walked up to Kyne in front of the stands shortly after the gates opened and said, "Looks like a big day; see all those people up there," and he pointed to a section in the grandstand. "Well," commented a man in uniform standing nearby, "I wouldn't count on much business from those people.

George Murphy, Kyne's friend from boyhood, who became a vaudeville entertainer and later one of Bill's racing officials.

That's a group that we have escorted here from the State Insane Asylum."

An incident not quite so amusing at the time occurred at the last of Kyne's two meetings at Juarez, just across the border from El Paso.

One day Bill received an order from a Mexican general demanding that the track pay a $2,500 daily "passport tax." This was in addition to taxes and fees already being paid to the government, and the new tax was sheer extortion.

"We were already losing money," said Kyne, and after paying the new tax for a few days we closed the meeting."

George Murphy, one of Bill's boyhood friends and a steward at Juarez, told of their departure.

"Bill and I shared a hotel room in El Paso. After the meeting closed we were waiting until time to go to the station to take a train home. Bill got a phone call and the caller tipped him off that two Mexican officers were on their way from Juarez to arrest him. Don't know whether it was because he had called off the meeting or because the last day's passport tax hadn't been paid.

"Bill and I started hurriedly packing our bags and hadn't finished when there was a loud knock on the door and a Mexican voice called, 'Mr. Kyne, Mr. Kyne.' We grabbed our bags and went down the fire escape. We took a taxi to the station and told the driver to let us out on the opposite side of the tracks from the station. We were afraid the officers might come to the station before the train left, so we got behind some trees and shrubs and when the train pulled in we boarded from the opposite side.

"We were waiting for the train to pull out when two Mexican officers came through the train paging, 'Mr. Kyne, Mr. Kyne.' We sat there in silence and then breathed a sigh of relief as the two men left and the train began to move out. Later Bill sent the hotel a check for our bill."

2

Bill Kyne was conducting a race meeting at Tulsa when I first met him. That was in the summer of 1930. I was working on the *Tulsa Tribune* and my job was to come in at 4:00 A.M. and get the early teletype news stories ready for the first edition. I got off at 1:00 P.M. and spent most of the afternoons at the races.

One day Kyne mentioned that his publicity man, Walter King, was leaving when the meeting closed to accept a job in the East and that he would have to find a replacement. He said he needed someone to handle publicity for a new meeting scheduled for early fall at Tanforan, near San Francisco. (The meeting was to run under the newly devised option system of betting.)

For a long time I had wanted to go to California, and when I asked for the job, Kyne said I could have it, and that I should report September 1.

Although Bill Kyne was to be general manager he had two partners in the Tanforan operation, John W. Marchbank and Joseph A. Murphy. When Bill returned from Tulsa late in August he learned his partners had already started preliminary arrangements and had hired a publicity man,

Oscar Otis. Oscar had previously covered the races in Tijuana for one of the San Diego papers.

When I arrived Kyne apologetically explained the situation and said he could give me a job as a mutuel clerk. Sensing my disappointment, Kyne said, "I've got an idea that might make you some money. In Chicago and New York they put out a scratch sheet that sells real well, and I think one might go over out here. I've got one at home that I'll show you."

I knew what a scratch pad was but had no idea what a scratch sheet was. The one Kyne showed me was a two-page publication that was printed early each racing day and listed the horses in each race in post position order with estimated odds, jockeys and weights, horses that had been scratched, track condition, and post time. The horse picked to win in each race was printed in bold type. Kyne said he would make a morning line (estimated odds) for me.

I said okay. I'd give it a try.

After giving the idea thought for several days I decided the scratch sheet wasn't giving the race players as much information as they would like. Why not, I thought, list the entire field in the order in which I predicted the horses would finish, with brief comment after each entrant? Kyne thought this an excellent suggestion, especially since racing would be new to most of the people at the track.

The little paper, which was named *The Blue Sheet*, went on sale at track entrances and with several sellers also inside extolling the publication's valuable information. It sold for twenty-five cents with ten cents going to the sellers.

Opening-day sales were a disappointment. So were those of the second day and the third day. The sellers were becoming discouraged and I wasn't making much above the printing bill. Then on the fourth day a combination of circumstances brought about a welcome change.

Kyne would phone me at the print shop each morning to

give me his odds for each horse. He would read them off rapidly, and in the third race that fourth day I got behind in taking them down, and as he called 20 for a horse I only put down 2, intending to add the 0 when I caught up.

Bill's line was used in listing the horses in order of predicted finish, the one with shortest odds would be first choice, second shortest next choice, and on down.

Hurrying to get my copy to the printer I forgot to add the omitted 0 on the 20-to-1 shot, a young filly named Miss Fashion Plate, and put her on top as 2-to-1 choice.

Looking over the sheet as the press run was finished, I was flabbergasted as I realized my mistake. I'd have to explain it to Kyne.

Shortly before post time a heavy downpour began, and the track was sloppy for the third race. Miss Fashion Plate's record offered little encouragement to a bettor, and it showed no mud races. But mud apparently was what Miss Fashion Plate had wanted. At the break she dashed to the front and drew away to win by five lengths for a payoff of $340 on $5 win tickets. That's 67 to 1. At Tanforan that meeting $5 was the least you could wager and there was no place or show betting.

After the race there were about 400 unsold scratch sheets and I told the sellers to go through the stands and pass them all out. Luckily *The Blue Sheet* had three more winners that day and five on top the following day. *The Blue Sheet* was now firmly established and money was rolling in.

Then I bought a half interest in a two-horse stable owned by Joe Whittingham. It wasn't a profitable venture, because one horse wasn't very sound and the other not very fast, and we sold the horses in less than a year. Our stable boy was Joe's sixteen-year-old brother, Charlie. For the last twenty years Charlie Whittingham has been one of the top trainers in America.

The scratch-sheet bonanza didn't last. Two years later

Oscar Otis was on the *San Francisco Chronicle* sports staff and assigned to cover the Tanforan meeting. He was succeeded at Tanforan by Lew Falk. Realizing the demand for the type of information *The Blue Sheet* carried, he persuaded Sports Editor Harry B. Smith to run a daily two-column handicap in the *Chronicle*, using the exact pattern of *The Blue Sheet*. Then the *Examiner, News,* and *Call-Bulletin* also began running graded handicaps, and so did the *Tribune* and *Enquirer* in Oakland.

The Blue Sheet sales gradually declined but still showed a profit. The following year Kyne sold his interest in Tanforan to John Marchbank, who took over as manager, and Marchbank decided the track should receive a concession fee from the tip sheets. In addition to *The Blue Sheet*, there was *The Hermit*, still being published, *The Yellow Sheet*, and *The Telegraph Handicap*. These only listed their first three choices in each race. All tip sheets were sold inside the track.

Marchbank asked for bids for the exclusive tip-sheet concession. For *The Blue Sheet* I turned in the high bid of fifty dollars per day, but my competitors were permitted to sell outside the gates. After one season of paying the concession fee, *The Blue Sheet* went out of business.

3

Kyne managed the Riverside Park Track near Kansas City in partnership with Tom Pendergast, a political power in Missouri and in the Democratic Party, and Phil McCrory. McCrory owned the track. Pendergast took care of the permit for pari-mutuel wagering in the county and bankrolled the venture. Kyne was given a free hand in running the meetings.

A man who was a close friend and political protégé of Pendergast was at the track one day, and the track announcer, Eddie Killian, invited him to watch a race from up in his booth. (In those days it was the custom of announcers to call only the first five or six horses in a race.)

The horses had reached the turn for home, and as Killian finished naming the leaders the crowd was startled to hear another voice come through over the public address system with the following words: "Where's that sonofabitch I bet on?"

The voice was that of the announcer's guest, a future president of the United States—Harry S. Truman.

Pendergast is credited with putting Truman in the White House.

Pendergast's young son, Tom, Jr., was at the track frequently. While gathering material for this book I wrote to him in Kansas City for some information. He phoned with what I wanted and added more:

"Kyne had a lot of capable people working for him. I remember watching his mutuel manager—I think his name was Sparks, yes, that's right, Art Sparks—add up a list of figures, and he was the fastest man with figures I ever saw. He was unbelievable, and Mickey Dwyer was another good one." (That was before the days of the totalizator machines, and all tabulations and calculations had to be done manually.)

"The track veterinarian was the best in the business," he continued. "He could just run his hands over a horse's legs and tell if he was sound.

"Edward Thornton was the presiding steward and he was real strict.

"They built a nice clubhouse at Riverside Park, but my father preferred a box in the grandstand, on the finish line. For many years he had a box on the finish line at Churchill Downs, and he would take me to see the Derby.

"Riverside was a good track—not real fast, but good soil, and very few horses broke down. Many trainers would condition their horses there and move on to Chicago and other big tracks. Ben Jones would race horses there under the care of his son Jimmy."

Riverside Park was the first recognized track that Johnny Adams rode on. After riding at bush tracks in Texas, he came to Kansas City in 1936 and was leading rider of the meeting. He moved to Longacres and was top rider. From there he went to Santa Anita, and the following year he was leading rider of America, and won the title again in 1942 and 1943.

Johnny Adams later became a trainer, and at the present time is trainer of J. O. Tobin, the first horse to beat Seattle Slew.

4

One of Bill Kyne's favorite vacation spots was Richardson Springs, a resort near Chico in northern California. One day in the spring of 1932, Kyne phoned me from there and said he had something important coming up and wanted to talk to me. "Drive up tomorrow afternoon, and plan to stay overnight," he said.

When I arrived Kyne said, "I'll show you around and we can talk business later." The resort was located in a beautiful setting of hills, trees, and volcanic boulders with a small mountain near the front of the three-story main building. Halfway up the mountain was a large painted cutout of an Indian in prone position drinking from a spring. The figure was made visible at night by an attractive lighting effect. It was used as the resort's logo.

One of Richardson Springs' attractions was its heralded health-giving mineral water—three types. There were mineral bath houses and three wells of drinking water, all of which tasted terrible. Across a nearby stream was a narrow foot suspension bridge that swayed and scared you when you walked across it. (Richardson Springs is now a retirement home.)

During dinner with Kyne and his wife nothing was mentioned about why he had sent for me, and I was becoming more curious. After dinner Kyne suggested we sit outside. It was a balmy, moonlit evening, and we sat beside a water fountain out front.

"The reason that I called you," Kyne began, "is that I've been giving a lot of thought the last few days to an idea and have decided to go ahead with it. I'm going to get a bill on the ballot in November to legalize pari-mutuel wagering on horse races in California. There'll be a lot of work to do. We'll need publicity and I want you to handle it."

Kyne went on to explain that while California had racing under the option system of betting, it wasn't a sound enough foundation to encourage the growth and expansion of the sport. The option system was merely a technicality to get around the existing law against betting on races. True, it had been ruled legal in court, but that was merely the opinion of one judge, and might be reversed in another court.

After two and a half years under the option system, no new tracks had been built, and racing was still conducted at only one track in California.

Kyne realized the sport needed a racing bill legalized by a vote of the people, or by the state legislature. That's what he was determined to bring into existence.

"If California gets pari-mutuel betting, it will become one of the top racing states in America, on par with New York, Florida, and Illinois. We would attract the best stables, horses, and riders. Los Angeles will become as big a racing center as New York, and that's where I want to build a track."

The city named for angels was then regarded by many as just a big hick town where farmers from Iowa and Nebraska retired and where crackpot cults thrived. San Francisco was known as an open town, a sporting town with big spenders and hordes of horse players that gave the bookies a big play.

I looked at Kyne quizzically, "Los Angeles?"

"Yes, Los Angeles has the population and it has the space to expand; San Francisco hasn't. With the climate down there, Los Angeles is going to grow. May become as large as New York City."

I asked if he thought there were enough gamblers there to support a track.

"Probably not," he replied, "but they'll learn to like racing. There's money in the movie industry, and I think those people would be good customers." After a moment's silence he added, "Racing would be big in Los Angeles, and you can bet on that."

Returning home two days later, Kyne's first move was to explain his plan to John Marchbank, his Tanforan partner, from whom he expected approval and strong financial support. He received neither.

Tanforan was doing nicely with two meetings a year under the option system, no competition, and Marchbank saw no reason to change things. He told Kyne he not only would not support such a racing bill, but would oppose it. It was the first of many disappointments in his quest for financial aid.

A few days later Kyne decided to pull out of Tanforan. It would now be difficult to work in harmony with Marchbank, and besides that he wanted to devote full time to his racing bill. Kyne asked Marchbank to buy his interest in Tanforan. Bill agreed to accept ninety thousand dollars, most of which was spent on his campaign for a new racing law.

Two factors made it difficult for Kyne to raise funds: a scarcity of money because of the depression; and the opinion of many that the bill didn't have much chance. He began using his money from the Tanforan deal.

Among the few supporting his efforts were the Pacific Coast Breeders' Association, Norman W. Church, an industrialist in Los Angeles and the owner of a Thoroughbred breeding farm, and Al Uniack.

The first move was to obtain the required number of signatures to get the racing referendum on the ballot, which many thought a task of doubtful success. Kyne rented offices in the Russ Building and organized a crew of signature-solicitors. By the end of August he had obtained 100,000 names in the Bay Area, and Church, heading the campaign in the south, secured 90,000, for a total well above the 110,000 required.

Now the real work began—the campaign for votes. In addition to publicity, advertising was scheduled for newspapers, billboards, and radio, and two million brochures were being prepared for mailing.

The slogan was "Save the Taxpayers a Million Dollars a Year. Vote Yes on 5." The ads claimed horse racing would produce a million a year in revenue for the state. To some that seemed an exaggerated claim, and although Kyne visualized a bright future for the sport, it is doubtful that in his wildest imagination he could have foreseen that by 1976 horse racing in California would produce a year's total of $96,645,115 for the state treasury.

The campaign was well underway and going smoothly when it received its first setback—opposition from William Randolph Hearst. The powerful Hearst newspapers came out with an editorial opposing the measure, and continued a relentless campaign urging its defeat.

There was a flaw in the wording of one paragraph in the bill, and when the papers discovered this, they made the most of it. The measure authorized the state to collect a tax of $1,500 for each day of racing. Because the single word *racing* was used instead of *Thoroughbred horse racing*, the Hearst papers contended that if the bill passed all types of racing, including foot races at college and high school

This sketch depicting Kyne carrying the load in his uphill campaign for racing was published in the New York Press, *a weekly sports tabloid, in 1933.*

track meets, would have to pay the $1,500 daily tax. A number of other papers began using this point as a basis of attack on the bill. Assurance that the bill would only tax horse racing was issued by Kyne, but much damage had already been done.

Even so, a straw poll showed that Proposition 5 was leading by a narrow margin.

The election date was November 8, and late in October Kyne's efforts were dealt another blow. Norman W. Church, a staunch supporter in the south, suddenly announced he was opposing the referendum, and persuaded several members of the Pacific Coast Breeders' Association to join him. The announcement received wide publicity in opposition papers.

It is not clear exactly what caused Church's reversal. One theory is that Church and some of his friends had concluded that the bill as written would give Kyne too much power—that it would give him virtual control of racing in California.

As election day, Tuesday, November 8, approached, Kyne and those of us who had worked with him were weary but hopeful.

There was no television to watch for election results, and radio didn't handle returns as it now does, and the only early news we got on election night was from calling the newspapers, and it was encouraging.

Early the next morning I unfolded the *Chronicle*, and my pulse quickened as I read the following headline: RACING BILL LEADING. Proposition 5 was ahead by 72,352 votes, 250,084 to 177,732, though only 2,172 precincts of the 10,547 total had been reported. Tabulation of votes was much slower in those days, and frequently it was two or three days before ballots from rural areas reached election headquarters. Yet the news story said the racing referendum seemed assured of victory.

I phoned Kyne. "Yep, we've won it," he said happily, although he didn't sound as jubilant as I had expected, but Kyne was not one to become overly emotional in either victory or defeat.

When the afternoon papers came out, they showed the racing bill's margin had been drastically cut, and it was now leading by only 268,960 to 263,454 with 5,098 precincts counted. The next morning, Thursday, the newspapers reported 9,293 precincts were in, and Proposition 5 trailing by 812,410 to 774,293. With 1,254 precincts yet to be heard from, there was still hope, but not much.

Thursday afternoon papers carried the complete and final results. The votes were: Yes, 904,840; No, 956,028. The bill had lost by only 51,188 votes out of a total of 1,860,868.

It was ironic that the measure had carried in all of the metropolitan areas where tracks would be built, and that its defeat had come from rural sections where the only way people there would be affected by racing was to benefit from taxes it would produce.

Kyne's disappointment was accentuated because of the early lead and the belief that he had won—and sixty thousand dollars of his own money had gone down the drain.

"You have to take the bitter with the sweet," he said.

Then he looked for the silver lining, and it was there, shining brightly. Due to the close vote on a bill that was claimed to have little chance, Kyne realized it would be a cinch. to get another bill approved in the near future.

"We'll try again, and next time we will win," he commented.

And he didn't wait long to start over again. He persuaded two friends, Assemblymen Bill Hornblower and Tom Maloney, to write a new and improved pari-mutuel racing bill. It was introduced in the state legislature's spring session by Maloney and Clare Woolwine.

It passed in the assembly by a fifty to twenty-nine vote

and in the senate twenty-two to sixteen. Governor James Rolph said he would sign it. But a few days later, April 28, 1933, Governor Rolph vetoed the bill.

Hornblower and Maloney contended the governor's action was due to pressure from Hearst.

Once again Kyne had to take the bitter. As usual he was undaunted and began another attempt. A special state election was coming up in June, and he succeeded in getting his racing bill on the ballot.

This time, instead of odds of 100 to 1, they were more like 3 to 5, and many jumped on the bandwagon.

On June 27, 1933, the bill passed by a vote of 792,106 to 475,540, nearly 2 to 1. (The heavier total vote in 1932 is explained by the fact that it was the first Roosevelt election.)

Less than eight months after his first disheartening defeat, Bill Kyne's dream of a pari-mutuel racing law for California had become a reality. But there was more bitter yet in store for the Irishman from South of Market Street.

5

The new racing law provided for the appointment of a three-member board to serve as a governing body for the sport. Governor Culbert Olson appointed Carleton F. Burke, William P. Roth, and John A. McNaughton as members of the California Horse Racing Board. Burke was elected chairman and W. Claude Buchanan was appointed secretary.

Under Burke's leadership the board drew up a rigid set of requirements that an applicant must meet to obtain a racing license. These were not announced and were unknown to seekers of a racing permit.

Kyne had organized the California Jockey Club, and with Al Uniack's assistance, now began looking for a site in the Los Angeles area. He took me with him when he went to look at a piece of property Uniack had located in Culver City. The price, Kyne decided, was excessive, in addition to some other drawbacks. Later we went south again to look at a possible site in El Monte, which Kyne deemed too small, and lacking in sufficient traffic outlets.

Meanwhile, Bill's friends and advisers in his hometown kept urging him to build his track in the San Francisco Bay Area—contending it would be a mistake to go south. He knew it would be difficult to get financing from his local contacts for a track in Los Angeles, and he was getting impatient. Anxious to get started, he began looking for a location in the north.

He looked at some East Bay property in San Pablo and took an option, though he wasn't entirely satisfied with the site. And there was strong local opposition to the building of a track there.

Kyne continued his search and learned the property of the old Curtis-Wright Airfield on the south side of San Mateo was for sale. He took an option and filed an application with the racing board to build a track to be known as Bay Meadows. The site had once been a meadow and was near the bay, hence the name.

(John O'Neill, a well-known Bay Meadows racegoer, recalls herding cows across what is now the track's infield when his parents owned the land and operated a dairy farm. They later sold it to Curtis-Wright.)

By the time Kyne submitted his application in early fall, the racing board had received ten other requests for permits. Licenses were sought by Hal Roach, the movie magnate, Jack Kearns and Gene Normile, former managers of Jack Dempsey, Harry Comstock, Pasadena hotelman, Lou Smith, head of Rockingham Park, and Joe Smoot, a racetrack promoter from Florida. Their applications didn't meet the board's stipulations and were denied.

With Kyne waiting for a go-ahead from the racing board to begin work, Dr. Charles H. Strub, a former dentist and at that time president and part owner of the San Francisco Seals baseball team, organized the St. Francis Jockey Club. He took an option on some land in the Ingleside district in San Francisco, and filed an application with the racing board.

At a meeting on October 13, the racing board issued the first permit for a new track in California—to Dr. Strub—and denied the application of Bill Kyne.

When Bill Hornblower heard the news he let out a howl that could be heard all the way from his San Francisco law offices at Third and Market to the Ferry Building. "I'll demand that the governor replace the racing board," he screamed. And later he did, to no avail. Kyne protested in a letter to the board, which said in part:

"I cannot understand why you have denied the application of the California Jockey Club. I feel that I have a thorough knowledge of horse racing and that I know how to conduct horse racing meets. I know that I can bring good stables and good riders to California, and that I feel sure I can do as much to elevate racing in this state as any other man."

Burke later explained the board was not turning down individuals as such, but organizations whose setups didn't meet the board's requirements. He intimated that if Kyne would make some changes and resubmit his application it would be approved.

It was reported that the board actually favored both Strub and Kyne—Strub because of the men and financing he had backing him, and Kyne because of his work on the racing bills.

Burke had not wanted a permit-seeker to raise money from scratch by getting a permit and then selling stock. He wanted a large amount of stock sold in advance and men with an established reputation in business and profession as officers of the association. "An applicant will have to get the right people in with him and the money in the bank," Burke stated.

A few days later Kyne had calmed down somewhat and announced he would make some changes and resubmit his application. But now he would have to look to the south again.

Tanforan, with a track already built, was reorganized by John W. Marchbank under the name of Tanforan Company,

Ltd., and had been granted permission for a 1933 fall meeting and a spring meeting the following year. And Strub now had the permit for Northern California's second track. Under the new law, one hundred days of racing would be allocated for both the north and south. Two tracks in each section could have fifty days apiece.

After Kyne had decided to build in the Bay Area, Al Uniack, a staunch believer in the south, decided to seek a permit of his own and had his eye on the Baldwin property. Kyne said he probably would go in with Uniack.

Meanwhile, Strub's announcement of plans to build in Ingleside evoked immediate and strong opposition from residents, who said they would fight Strub's efforts to get a rezoning ordinance passed. They began organizing to take their fight to the city supervisors, who were said to look with disfavor on a track within the city limits.

Strub had no desire to complicate things further by becoming involved in zoning fights that had only a slight chance of success.

He informed the racing board that he was relinquishing his permit, and that he planned to submit an application for a track in the Los Angeles area.

It appeared certain that Strub would get his permit in the south, and that meant Kyne would have to turn back to the north again.

On November 15, Bill Kyne informed the board he had reorganized, obtained adequate financing, and would shortly request a license to go ahead in San Mateo.

Meanwhile Hal Roach had formed the Los Angeles Turf Club and applied for a permit to build a track on the old Lucky Baldwin estate near Arcadia. He had been turned down previously for lack of proper financing.

With Strub looking for a location, Leigh Battson, an oil company executive, brought Strub and Roach together. One had an acceptable organization; the other a site. They joined forces, with Strub slated as the head of Santa Anita Park, later to become one of America's most renowned and successful racetracks.

Racing under the new law, however, already had returned to the state. The first racing with pari-mutuel wagering was at the San Joaquin County Fair at Stockton in the fall of 1933. Racing followed at the county fair at Pomona and at Tanforan.

In order to help racing get off to a good start, Kyne loaned his equipment to the fairs and supplied his experienced crew, which he had used at the Gresham meeting that closed shortly before Stockton opened. He also served as supervisor without remuneration.

The recently invented totalizator had not yet reached the west, and Kyne's mutuel machines were used. These were only a register of bets. They were a metal contraption about two feet wide and four feet high. One was placed behind each mutuel clerk, who sold preprinted tickets from a rack. Another man, called a clicker, manned the mutuel machine. As tickets were sold the seller would call out to the clicker the ticket number and the clicker would pull a lever to record it on the register, which totaled the tickets sold on each horse. The balance of necessary compilation of figures was done by human calculators, among whom were Art Sparks, Mickey Dwyer, and Willie Kyne.

Calculators would take a reading about every five minutes and figure each horse's odds. These were phoned across the track to a man who would hang them up on the odds board.

6

In contrast to the opposition Kyne encountered in the East Bay and Strub in San Francisco, the building of Bay Meadows received a cordial welcome from the San Mateo city officials and the Chamber of Commerce.

They realized the community would benefit from the track. The name *San Mateo* would receive national publicity through news stories in sports pages throughout the country; the track would be a large city taxpayer; it would bring people from other towns who would spend money at service stations, restaurants, and stores; it would create jobs and bring in horse owners, trainers, jockeys, and stable help who would need lodging and would spend money with local merchants.

Bay Meadows' ground-breaking ceremonies on April 8, 1934, were attended by more than one hundred people. On hand were Mayors A. R. Cotton of San Mateo, C. A. Buck of Burlingame, and Robert G. Hooker of Hillsborough, and Chamber of Commerce Presidents Thomas Hunt of San Mateo and A. H. Sagehorn of Burlingame. William P. Roth represented the California Horse Racing Board.

Mayor Cotton spoke of past racing in the state and com-

Bay Meadows under construction in 1934.

mented on the time when Leland Stanford bred and raced some of the finest horses in the world. In the name of San Mateo he welcomed the California Jockey Club and Bay Meadows.

A few days before the track opened Kyne was the guest of honor at a dinner given by citizens of San Mateo at the Benjamin Franklin Hotel to celebrate the coming of a new industry. It was attended by more than two hundred, and Mayor Cotton was master of ceremonies. Among the speakers was Peter B. Kyne, the noted author whom Bill Kyne had made president of the California Jockey Club. Peter B. and Bill were distant relatives.

On the morning of opening day, November 3, 1934, Bill Kyne arrived early. He walked out front, turned, viewed the plant, and commented: "There it is."

The track that Kyne built. Bay Meadows as it stands today.

It was the fruition of his years of dreaming, planning, espousing the cause of the Thoroughbred to the voters of California, and giving his time and his money without stint.

After two years of enduring many frustrations and bitter disappointments Bill Kyne was now enjoying "the sweet."

"This is just the beginning," he said. "There are improvements to be made, and I'm looking forward to the time we can offer minimum purses of one thousand dollars and handicaps that will attract the best horses in the country."

The opening had been diligently promoted, and a special train brought customers from Los Angeles, including many from the movie industry. Movie star Wallace Beery and Mrs. William P. Kyne cut the ribbon, officially opening the plant.

Adding color to the inaugural ceremonies were San Mateo

Actor Wallace Beery and Mrs. William P. Kyne, cutting ribbon at Bay Meadows' opening ceremonies.

County's famous Sciot Band and the California Greys marching band. The Gymkhana Club escorted racing judges to their stand in a tallyho.

Society editors from San Francisco covered the event, and Babette, *Examiner* fashion editor, devoted a column to the opening, and began her story:

"The opening of the peninsula's new race course, Bay Meadows, came as a challenge yesterday to San Francisco and peninsula society to dress up in the high style standards traditional with the ultra-smart crowds that frequent Auteil, Longchamps, Ascot and Belmont Park.

"Local society met the challenge by turning out in its best attire."

The San Mateo Times commented: "Opening day spectators realized that Bay Meadows' inaugural season actually signalizes the return of horse racing to California. Today's crowds saw the first new track built for vision and comfort since the people of California voted for the revival of racing.

"All eyes were pinned on the totalizator, a $250,000 device, first on the West Coast; the electrically operated machine that records on the giant board in the infield the amount of money wagered on each horse, the total pool and the mutuel payoffs."

The first day's attendance was fifteen thousand and the mutuel handle for eight races was $117,753. (Nine-race programs were not adopted until several years later.) There was no daily double or exacta betting, because the tote machine could then handle only win, place, and show wagers.

Among the opening-day crowd at Bay Meadows was a sixteen-year-old youth named Bob Strub, and forty-three years later at a turf dinner he mentioned that it was the first time he had seen a horse race and that he remembered the horse's name that won the first race. It was Rapid Bell. Strub's parents then lived in Menlo Park, near the track.

Robert P. Strub later became president and general manager of Santa Anita, the track his father built, and served two terms as president of the prestigious Thoroughbred Racing Associations of North America.

Turf writers covering the initial meeting were Abe Kemp for the *Examiner*, Oscar Otis for the *Chronicle*, Jack McDonald for the *Call-Bulletin*, Tom Laird for the *News*, Lee Owen for the *Oakland Tribune*, Tom Beebe for the *Oakland Enquirer*, and J. J. Murphy for the *Daily Racing Form*.

The $25,000 added Bay Meadows Handicap was the season's feature, and it was won by Frank Carraud's Time Supply. The meeting closed on December 16, averaging a little under $100,000 in daily wagers.

Off-track betting has been legalized in New York and is a controversial issue in other states with racing, but it is not new. A form of off-track betting was introduced by Kyne at the first Bay Meadows meeting.

He arranged for Western Union and Postal Telegraph to install teletype machines in a room next to the mutuel department and receive money-order bets placed at any of the telegraph companies' branch offices. Wagers had to be filed one hour before post time. Money orders were wired back to the winners.

The track averaged more than four thousand dollars per day in wire bets, and with a daily handle of under one hundred thousand dollars, that was a sizable amount. Santa Anita installed the same system, but near the end of its first season, the racing board obtained a ruling from the attorney general declaring the system illegal, and it was discontinued.

Following the close of Bay Meadows, most of the Bay Meadows horses went south for the Santa Anita meeting that opened on Christmas Day before a crowd of 30,000, who wagered $258,961 on the eight-race card. On the second day only 4,824 spectators attended, and the total handle was $84,164. The third day it was $94,775.

One of Bill Kyne's self-appointed advisers snickered and said, "I told you so."

"Give them time," Bill replied. "They're not horse players down there yet, but they will be." And he was right. Business gradually began to pick up, and Santa Anita had a successful season.

7

Kyne's private office was far from private, and how he got any work done was a constant amazement to his friends. His front door was almost always open, and it opened into the front office, through which a person had to pass to reach other offices.

When an acquaintance would pass by and look in, Kyne would motion for him to come in. It wasn't unusual for three or four visitors to be sitting in Bill's office as he handled phone calls, tried to talk to someone there on a business appointment, or dictated letters.

Occasionally when things got a bit hectic he would comment, "This place is a madhouse, isn't it?" and then with a grin add, "But I love it."

One day between racing seasons I walked into Kyne's office and he was sitting alone going through some papers. After a few minutes he got up, put on his hat, and said, "I'm getting out of here, it's too quiet to get any work done."

He had a private bar adjoining his office, and as quitting time approached he would mix a Scotch highball for himself and for the two women in the front office—his secretary,

Mae De Vol, secretary to Bill Kyne, and to his three successors.

Mae Feist (now Mrs. Frank De Vol), and a typist named Evelyn. With two drinks in his hand he would peek around the door to make sure no one else was around, and once commented with a twinkle in his eyes, "I wouldn't want your boss to catch you girls drinking on the job."

During one busy week there were days when the women didn't want their drinks but wouldn't say so. They hid them in a desk drawer, and one day Kyne walked by when Evelyn had left her drawer pulled out and Bill spotted three untouched highballs. "Well, Evelyn, I see you're getting behind with some of your assignments."

After that when Mae and Evelyn didn't want their drinks (he made them too strong) they poured them into a nearby planter box containing a large green plant. The plant thrived on Johnnie Walker Black Label and may have become the first alcoholic houseplant.

Kyne was a stickler for proper language when his secretary or any other woman was in his office, and he wouldn't permit the telling of an off-color joke. And even when no woman was present I never heard him tell one himself, or use a profane or vulgar word, though he would chuckle over a good risqué story told by someone else.

If a man even used the word *hell* or *damn* when one of the women who worked in his office was present he would put up his hand and caution, "Now, now, watch your language, there's a lady present." Though he never got to be ordained, in many respects he was a priest at heart.

Bill Kyne was an avid answerer of letters. "Every letter received an answer if he could find any conceivable reason to reply," said Mae. "Sometimes all there was to say would go into one sentence. If someone had sent a letter offering to sell him the Golden Gate Bridge, he probably would have answered it."

There was one time, though, that Kyne didn't want to answer a letter. It was from a man whose name I can't recall, so I'll use the name Nesbitt. He was a shareholder and a chronic complainer. This time, as usual, his criticism was unjustified. As Kyne finished reading the letter, Bill Hornblower walked in and Kyne said, "Here's another letter from that guy Nesbitt. This time *you* can answer it."

The track's vice-president said, "Yeah, let me have it. I'll put the SOB in his place." He started dictating to Kyne's secretary, and twice after several paragraphs he started over again, and the more he tried to explain the madder he got. He got up and began walking the floor and biting down on his cigar. After dictating a full page, he still wasn't satisfied and said, "No, throw that away, he doesn't deserve that much answer. Take this:

William B. (Bill) Hornblower and Kyne.

Dear Mr. Nesbitt:

Your letter received and contents noted. To hell with you.

Sincerely,

William B. Hornblower,
Vice-President

Another amusing incident concerning Hornblower occurred when he was a state assemblyman. Assemblyman Tom Flynn had asked Hornblower and Tom Maloney to join his side on a controversial bill. When the bill came up for debate, Hornblower rose and began talking against it. Maloney, seated next to him, began trying to get his attention, but Hornblower ignored him. Frantic, Maloney pulled on his coattail and whispered, "Bill, Flynn is *for* the the bill." Without the slightest hesitation, Hornblower said, "Now that I've told you what's bad about this bill, I'll tell what's good about it," and he went on to give a convincing discourse. The bill passed, and Hornblower was complimented in the press for his fairness in presenting both sides of a bill he was supporting.

Hornblower was in Kyne's office one day and commented on the record season Santa Anita had just concluded.

Kyne said: "Just think of all the money we would have if we had gotten a track down south."

In a sardonic tone Hornblower said: "Yeah, just think of all the money *you* would have had to *give away*."

Kyne was considerate and tactful when issuing written instructions or demands. When the night watchman complained that some of the press-box bunch had been staying in the press bar long after the races, Kyne posted the following notice:

TO THE MEMBERS OF THE PRESS BOX:
Gentlemen:

Please be advised that the Press Box will be closed from this day on at 7:30 P. M. and not at 11:30 P. M. as happened Saturday night. On Saturday evenings the members of the press will be expected to leave the Press Box by 9:30 P. M. The fire danger to the grandstand is great when some of the lads have too much Coca Cola.

Wm. P. Kyne
General Manager

Kyne was an early riser. He lived in the San Francisco Marina district near the bay and would get up at five o'clock. For exercise he would walk across the Golden Gate Bridge and back before breakfast. During his walks he apparently kept his mind busy thinking up new ideas and things for his staff to do, and at seven o'clock he would call Mae, Eddie Benn, the track secretary, or me or all of us with instructions for the day.

Many a morning after being out late we groaned from being awakened by a call from the boss. We never did figure out why he couldn't have waited until we came to the office at nine.

Kyne regarded his close and loyal employees as though they were members of his family and thought nothing of asking us to work long hours, at times until late at night. And though there was no extra pay, we never complained. Each of us had much admiration and respect for the man. But when Bill had extra tickets for shows, sports events, and other functions, his office help was the first to get them.

Known as a man who was generous and loose with his money, Kyne oddly was not a big tipper. I've seen him leave a dollar tip when he took three of us to lunch and the bill was about twenty dollars.

His favorite luncheon spots were Bondy's, until it closed in the mid-fifties, and the Villa Chartier. Among his favorite restaurants for dinner were Uncle Tom's Cabin in San Bruno and Roberts-At-The-Beach. Uncle Tom's was the scene of many enjoyable after-the-races dinner parties with Kyne as the host.

When Emerson Murfee remodeled the Villa Chartier, he named one of the private dining rooms the Kyne Room, and Bill bought and donated expensive furnishings for it.

8

Bill Kyne was married twice. His marriage in 1918 to Myrtle Kerr ended in divorce in 1924. There were no children.

While racing at Salt Lake City in 1927, he met an attractive divorcee named Dorothy Moyle. Bill and Dorothy were married in 1928 at the Riverside Hotel in Reno (George Murphy was best man) and moved into an apartment in San Francisco. Dorothy had a young daughter, Marylin, whom Kyne later adopted.

It proved a good marriage, a happy marriage for both, though Dorothy had understandable difficulty adjusting to her husband's lack of conservatism in handling money. He was a big spender, a big gambler; he would give money away, loan it, and at times lose on his business ventures.

Yet, Bill Kyne sometimes was not generous with spending money for his wife.

"He was generous concerning big things," said Marylin, "but would get upset over little things like household expenses. He thought my mother bought too many things that were wasteful. But he wanted her to look nice and didn't object to her buying nice clothes."

However, Mrs. Kyne soon worked out a solution to her

spending-money problem. "Quite often when Bill went to sleep," said Marylin, "she took large bills from his pocket and he never missed them, but if she touched any of his change he would know it next morning and raise a big fuss. Actually my mother was quite frugal and she saved a lot of money."

Bill didn't like shopping, and his wife bought all of his clothes and decided what he would wear each day.

Another thing that Mrs. Kyne had to get used to was that her husband made their home his office away from his office, and the phone often was busy before and after working hours.

"He liked the telephone," commented his daughter. Marylin laughed as she recalled the times when the phone would ring during a meal and Kyne would tell Dorothy to say he wasn't home. "Then, after she had said he wasn't in and he learned the caller was a friend, he would jump up and take the phone before Mother could hang up."

Marylin was about four years old when her mother took her to the races at Kyne's Salt Lake City track, and it was there she met Bill for the first time.

"The first thing he said was 'How would you like an ice cream soda?' and oh, I thought that was just wonderful. But several races went by and I thought well, here's a man that promises but doesn't do what he promises. Then a little later a waiter came to our box with a big, beautiful ice cream soda.

"I guess ice cream sodas aren't easy to get at a racetrack. He may have had to send out for it."

Shortly after their marriage Mrs. Kyne wanted to buy a home but Bill didn't.

"He didn't want to be disturbed—just wanted to stay put," said Marylin. "Maybe it was because when he was young they had to move a lot. He had a fetish about it. Then when my mother's uncle died, he left her some money and she made a down payment on the home on Casa Way, but Dad still didn't want to move. Mother told him it was really a nice place, and he wouldn't have to bother with the moving. She had the movers come in early in the morning, and when Dad came home that night everything was in place and he loved it. He loved the fireplace and kept it going a lot."

Few people living knew the personal side of Bill Kyne as well as his adopted daughter, and she discussed him freely as we sat in her living room.

"He had compassion for people. He had been poor and he knew what it was like. He didn't like pomposity, and there was something about him that no matter who some people felt they were, they suddenly became natural because he was so at ease with everyone and they felt completely comfortable.

"He had a sense of humor and he was a vivacious type of person. When he came home everything came alive, and even the little dog hopped up and down, delighted to see him.

"He slept well. He said, 'I sleep well because I have a clear conscience.' He was an optimist, and he loved this country. His favorite TV programs were Westerns, and "The Cisco Kid" and "Hopalong Cassidy" were his favorites.

"He was so sweet to my mother—and to me. There wasn't a jealous bone in his body. He wasn't petty. If he got angry he exploded and then it was over with.

"Not every man would take a child not his own and raise it and love it as his own, but he was like that. I never felt I had any other father. He was just darling. We traveled a lot and had a wonderful time—going to places where he was racing, and he took me, if I wasn't in school, because he

57

wanted me to be with my mother.

"When I had to take medicine Dad would say, 'Well, there's nothing to it' and Mother would say, 'Well, you take it and show her' and he would take it first. Very sympathetic.

"He liked activity, and about the only time he really relaxed was when he went to Richardson Springs. He liked nature and enjoyed looking at the trees and the birds and the clouds. In the clouds he would imagine seeing lambs, lions, and other figures. He got a lot out of life and he enjoyed living."

A member of the Kyne household on Casa Way was a Sealyham terrier that was given to Marylin by D. J. Davis, a Bay Meadows director and the man who had owned the great Phar Lap. Winkie and Kyne formed an affectionate relationship, and the little dog slept on Bill's bed. Several times Kyne complained that his sleep was disturbed because the dog took up most of the bed. "He could have pushed her off but he didn't," Marylin said with a chuckle. "He was very fond of her. Winkie had a habit of barking when the doorbell rang, and there were times when she just barked and Dad thought he didn't hear the bell (he had developed a slight hearing deficiency) and he would get up and go to the door, and Mother and I would smile when he came back and said, 'Well, that dog is getting cuckoo.'"

I asked if he had any favorite sayings or adages other than the one about the bitter and the sweet.

"Yes: 'A still tongue is a wise tongue'—which he never followed himself," laughed Marylin. "But sometimes he would quote it to my mother when he thought she was talking too much."

"Why did Bill seldom drive his own car?" I asked (Don Blair and later Ralph Cunningham were his hired drivers, though he never referred to them as chauffeurs).

"Well," chuckled Marylin, "he wasn't a very good driver.

Bill Kyne; Winkie; daughter, Marylin; and wife, Dorothy.

But it was mostly because he could accomplish more by having someone else drive. He would read his mail and newspapers in the car, and if his secretary was with him, he would dictate letters. His mind was on things other than driving."

I asked Marylin if there was any particular or unusual incident concerning Kyne that stood out in her mind.

"Yes. I was seventeen and we were at Del Mar and I went swimming at the beach. Dad had the gout and a swollen ankle and came down to the beach in a wheelchair, but he got in the shallow water. They thought the water would be good for him.

"I was standing out a little way from the beach with the water about up to my shoulders, and I felt something touching my legs. I looked down and saw a big mass of loose seaweed or kelp. Then a strong riptide caused me to lose my footing and started dragging me out. Dad called for me to come back and I yelled that I couldn't.

"The seaweeds got wrapped all around my legs—they were just like rope—and the waves got ferocious and I could feel the undertow. I struggled frantically because I knew I was being pulled out to sea. I was terribly frightened. I thought I was gone. Then I saw Dad coming after me. It was so wonderful because he didn't think of his own safety or the pain he must have felt.

"He swam out to me and grabbed my arm, and then we were both being pulled out to sea, but he got us balanced off each other and he had the strength to pull us back. I thought it was just marvelous that he had the courage and strength to rescue me. He saved my life. He was a very brave person.

"Mother had watched from the beach and she was as badly frightened as I was. When Dad was praised by some other people on the beach, he treated it lightly, as though it was nothing special. He was just darling."

Kyne kept in good physical condition through exercise, and it was due to his fitness that he was able to perform the rescue feat. He had been handball champion of the Olympic Club, and in addition to his morning walks across the Golden Gate Bridge, he and his wife played golf almost every Sunday morning at the Olympic Club's Lake Merced course.

9

Whether "characters" and colorful personalities were drawn to Kyne or whether he was drawn to them is a question, but Bay Meadows had a plethora of both—in a variety of jobs.

Eddie Benn, a peppy, jovial little Irishman, probably was known to more bartenders than any man in the Bay Area. And he had a mania for passes—to give away. When he went into a bar where he wasn't known, he would introduce himself, proudly announcing, "I'm Eddie Benn, secretary of the California Jockey Club." Most bartenders had never heard of such a club and were unimpressed, thinking he was a guy who took dictation and did typing for a club of jockeys.

But Eddie soon set them straight, then asked, "Would you like to have some passes to Bay Meadows?"

At the track Benn would go to the offices that had passes and beg and plead for just a few, then give them to strangers sitting next to him at a bar.

Eddie's honesty was never questioned, unless passes were involved, but leaving him alone in an office with passes on the desk was like leaving an alcoholic in a room with a bottle when he hadn't had a drink for a week.

Eddie was a friend of Ty Cobb, who lived alone in a nice

home down the peninsula not far from Bay Meadows. When the retired baseball star came to the track, Eddie would take him to the press box, which greatly pleased Cobb because there the drinks were free.

Ty Cobb's propensity for holding on to his money is well known, and when he and Eddie went to a bar, Eddie considered himself fortunate if he could talk his friend into buying one round to his three.

One evening when they were at a bar, Eddie suggested they go to a restaurant for dinner. Cobb (a multimillionaire) said it would be cheaper to go to his house and he would fix dinner.

"I was hungry and didn't want to go there," said Eddie, "but Ty insisted. When we got there all Ty could scrape up was some eggs and some moldy bread. He scrambled the eggs and scraped the mold off the bread and toasted it. I ate the eggs but not the moldy toast. After I left I went to a restaurant and had a good dinner."

Eddie also mentioned that Cobb poured them a drink— from a bottle of the cheapest bourbon on the market.

A colorful personality on Kyne's staff in the pre-Bay Meadows days was "Sec" Morrison. His full name was Maynard Hayward Morrison but his co-workers called him Sec. He had been a schoolteacher in El Reno, Oklahoma, and before that he lived in Salinas, Kansas, and played a horn in the town band. How a man with a background like that got to be a racing secretary is something I never learned.

He was a bachelor, but he liked the ladies. I first met him at the Kansas City race meeting of 1931 and estimated his age as somewhere in the forties.

Morrison was a man of medium build with a slightly balding head of brown hair and a somewhat thin, slow voice. Frequently during a conversation he'd make odd movements with his lower jaw while trying to adjust his ill-fitting false teeth.

Yet Sec would have a date four or five nights a week, and he had a host of gal friends—most of them much younger than himself and some quite attractive.

How and where he got them is a mystery that has never been solved. Even Solly Tichner couldn't find out, and Solly considered himself a super snooper. Solly was in charge of the printing and sale of programs.

What Solly did find out, though, is what went on—to some extent—when Morrison took a date to his room. At Kansas City a popular hotel with the racing crew was the Dixon, a medium-priced hostelry whose rooms could not honestly be advertised as sound-proof. One racing season Solly and Sec happened to get rooms across the hall from each other. Whenever Solly heard Morrison enter his room, he crossed the hall and put his ear to the door. If the elderly lothario had a woman with him, Solly listened, and next day he would gleefully give us a detailed report on what was said and what he envisioned occurred. Kyne was amused as much as the rest of us.

Solly and Sec Morrison had a common interest in the fair sex, but as a woman chaser Solly wasn't as successful, and it's likely he was envious—and hoped he could learn something from spying on the amorous racing secretary.

Morrison took the ribbing he received good naturedly. He was a good racing secretary and well liked by horsemen and co-workers. He handled his job with only one assistant, C. C. Paul. Later at Bay Meadows when racing became bigtime, Kyne occasionally complained about the large staff in the racing office, mentioning how Morrison managed with a single helper.

At Kansas City one day Morrison lost five hundred dollars entrusted to him by a trainer who put up the money to claim a horse. Sec put the five one-hundred-dollar bills in a back pocket where he had several programs on which he had marked horses he thought would win. While taking

M. H. (Sec) Morrison.

the money to the bookkeeper, he met one of his lady friends and handed her a program. When he reached the book-keeper's office, he didn't have the five hundred dollars. Worried, Morrison reported to Kyne, explaining he must have dislodged the bills when he gave away the program, but said he'd make good the loss.

Kyne said, "Forget it, the track will make it up." Then with a smile he added, "Next time be more careful when you are giving something to your lady friends."

Ed Barlow is another who could amuse Kyne. Courteous, soft-spoken, and articulate, Ed Barlow could have passed for a preacher. Instead, he was a racetrack cashier and a pool shark. Kyne enjoyed accompanying him to a poolroom and watching him perform. Barlow would get into a game, lose

Eddie Benn.

Mickey Curran.

Ed Barlow.

two or three small bets, and then his game would suddenly improve. He'd make difficult shots and appear greatly surprised, and comment on his remarkable run of luck as Kyne stood back and chuckled.

Ed was a trick-shot expert and a master with the cue, but he wasn't a slicker. He never played for big money, and after gaining back his losses and winning a few dollars, he would quit. He played for fun.

Mickey Curran is remembered for his natty attire and

disapproval of changing style. Mickey first worked for Kyne as a mutuel clerk, and after Bay Meadows was a few years old, his job was escorting people to the winner's circle for the winner-crowning routine. He also made a handicap chart for the *Call-Bulletin*.

Mickey came to the track each day in a neatly pressed suit, highly polished shoes, and a fresh shirt with cuff links given to him by actor Mickey Rooney. He wore shoes with French toes and in the summer a straw sailor hat. When both went out of style he had them ordered from the factory.

Mickey had come from the East and claimed it was from him that Damon Runyon got the idea for one of his fictional characters, the Lemon Drop Kid.

Some of the colorful personalities at Kyne's tracks also had colorful names, including Duck In and Duck Out, Dirty Shirt Sullivan, The Sheik, Lying Tom, Geronimo, and English Jack Bates.

Geronimo (John Wright) and Lying Tom (Tom O'Farrell) were given their nicknames by Bob Wuerth, who succeeded me as publicity director at Bay Meadows in 1959 when I went into the advertising business for a few years.

Geronimo, a black man, claimed he was an Indian and entitled to land in Oklahoma but was unable to get the government to hand it over. He was the press-box messenger. Once when I returned to my office at the track after briefly leaving it unoccupied, I stood at the door and watched Geronimo as he looked through a file cabinet drawer. When asked what he was looking for he replied: "Oh, uh, the mimeograph machine."

One of Geronimo's duties was to take photos to the San Francisco newspapers. One afternoon Bob Wuerth gave him a picture for the *Chronicle* and another for the *Call-Bulletin*, an afternoon paper.

Early next morning the *Call-Bulletin* sports editor phoned

Bob and said he had space for the picture but hadn't received it. When Geronimo came to work Bob asked why he hadn't delivered the photo. Geronimo looked puzzled and Wuerth said, "I told you to take pictures to two places. The *Chronicle* got theirs but the *Call-Bulletin* didn't. Why didn't you take the picture to the other paper?"

Geronimo thought for a moment.

"Oh, I guess I just forgot."

"You forgot!" yelled Bob, "How could you forget?"

"Well," countered Geronimo, as though he were being unjustly reprimanded, "you can't expect a man to remember everything."

Maybe it wasn't such a weak excuse at that. The angry Wuerth couldn't keep from laughing.

Amusing incidents around a racetrack are not uncommon, and Neil (Dirty Shirt) Sullivan was involved in one at Kyne's Portland track. Sullivan, who was given his nickname by turf writer Abe Kemp, is the trainer of a small stable. Usually his horses run in low-price claiming races, but once he had a stake horse that upped his prestige as a trainer.

During a Portland Meadows meeting Kyne received a telegram from San Francisco informing him that the sender would arrive in Portland that afternoon on Flight 42, and it was signed "Sullivan."

Thinking the wire was from Prescott Sullivan, the *Examiner's* ace sports columnist, Kyne sent his driver, Ralph Cunningham, to pick him up and bring him to the track. Kyne reserved a choice Club House table at which his guest would have dinner on the house before the night races started.

When the plane arrived Prescott Sullivan wasn't on it— but Dirty Shirt Sullivan was. Cunningham asked the arriving Sullivan if he had sent the wire. He had. (I was unable to learn why he sent it.) When Ralph brought Neil to the track Kyne ignored the mixup, and Dirty Shirt received the attention and service at the dinner table that would have been accorded the noted journalist.

Before every race Neil is confident he knows the winner, and he'll gladly share his knowledge with anyone who'll listen. Occasionally one of his selections wins at a big price, and then he chides everyone for not having bet on it. But to bet on all of Neil's selections would be about as practicable as flushing your money down the toilet and hoping some of it floats back up.

Duck In and Duck Out was another Bay Meadows character. He was a short, chubby little Irishman whose real name was Patrick Slavin, and he had been raised in New York's Bowery. His job at the track was delivering programs and overnight entries to various departments and other messenger assignments.

Slavin was given his odd nickname after telling of the following incident:

"I went to a circus but didn't have any money, and I crawled under the tent, and when I stood up I was right next to a guard. The guard looked at me and said, 'How did you get in here?' and I said, 'Oh, I just ducked in.' The guard said, 'Well, just duck out.'"

George Schilling, the presiding steward, gave Duck In his old suits and paid for having them altered, and one of them was solid green. It became his St. Patrick's Day suit, and his accessories for that day were all green—hat, shoes shirt, socks, tie, and four-leaf clover.

Duck In was not averse to taking things that didn't belong to him—passes, photos, or anything he might want.

In a bar one day I noticed a display of racing photos that had been missing from the publicity office for several weeks. The bar owner said he bought them from Duck In. I said, "Oh," and let it go at that.

In his later years, though, Duck In reformed and became a self-appointed Santa Claus to several persons he especially liked.

For many weeks before Christmas Duck In was frequently seen in downtown San Mateo with a large shopping bag and buying yule gifts. Each person on his list received from six to ten gifts, presented gift-wrapped in a shopping bag.

Duck In was seventy-four when hit by a car while crossing a street against a red light, and he died a few hours later. Joe Cohen, then Bay Meadows' general manager, informed the funeral home he would pay all expenses. At services for Duck In the funeral parlor was filled, much to the surprise of the mortician, who had commented when the body arrived that there wouldn't be many people at this funeral.

10

Kyne was a gambler at heart. In addition to gambling on his business ventures and horse races, he would bet on football and baseball games, a poker hand or a golf match, on the total of the day's wagering at the track, and once he bet on whether a horse could swim across the Golden Gate.

His bet on the swimming horse was made with Richie (Shorty) Roberts. Richie and his brother Wilford owned an old and well-known San Francisco restaurant named Roberts-At-The-Beach. Sophie Tucker, a famous singer of years past, got her start there.

One evening in 1938, Kyne was dining at the restaurant and Richie was telling Bill what a great swimmer his horse Blackie was. Richie and the horse frequently swam together in the ocean. Kyne contended that no horse was a good swimmer. Bristling, Roberts said, "Blackie can swim across the Golden Gate."

"That's ridiculous," retorted Kyne.

Want to bet?"

"Yes," was Kyne's instant reply.

The bet was reported to be one thousand dollars, though it's doubtful it was that much. Richie hardly could afford the loss of one thousand dollars, because only recently his restaurant had been in financial difficulties and Kyne had helped him save it by giving him the catering concession in the Bay Meadows Turf Club and Club House. But whatever the amount, the bet was on.

Blackie, twelve years old, was a former harness racer and still had stamina in his strong legs. He had been given to Roberts by George Gianinni, brother of the founder of the Bank of America.

Richie put Blackie into training, taking him to Hunters Point on the bay and swimming him out to Shad Rock, about half a mile off shore. The round trip was about equal to the distance across the Gate.

On October 1 they were ready. The starting place was Lime Point on the Marin side, and the destination just below Crissy Field.

On hand was a group of photographers and reporters, a horde of spectators, and an official of the SPCA. Also a tugboat with a boom to pick up Blackie if he couldn't make it, and Coast Guard vessels to give the horse a clear lane.

To show the horse the right direction a row boat went ahead with a slack rope tied to Blackie's halter. And the rope could be used to hold the animal's head up if he began to flounder.

A condition of the bet was that Richie was to accompany his horse, holding onto his tail, and wearing a life preserver.

Once underway, Blackie followed the pilot boat with the same strong, rhythmic leg strokes he had used in trotting races. As Blackie neared the shore Kyne joined the crowd in rooting for Blackie to make it. And make it he did. When the four-legged swimmer climbed out of the water he wasn't breathing as heavily as his owner.

Blackie's time of twenty-three minutes and fifteen seconds wasn't far behind the record at that time for swimming the

Blackie swimming across the Golden Gate.

gate—twenty minutes and fourteen seconds, set by Walter Pomeroy in 1914.

Though he had lost his bet, Bill Kyne celebrated Blackie's feat that night as host to a group of friends at a champagne and steak dinner at Roberts-At-The-Beach, with Blackie as guest of honor. The hero was brought in to nibble on a bale of hay placed on a dance-floor table.

Another unusual Bill Kyne bet was the one he made on a "sure thing" in a race at Bay Meadows. In the eighth race that day was a three-horse entry trained by R. H. McDaniel, then America's leading trainer. Any one of the three, if running uncoupled, would have been an outstanding favorite. Opposing the entry were only four other horses, making it a five-horse field as far as betting was concerned.

Earlier in the day Kyne had bet one hundred dollars with Solly Tichner on the total he predicted would be wagered on the day's program. With the eighth race coming up the

Richie (Shorty) Roberts, Kyne, and Blackie at celebration dinner.

handle on the previous races hadn't been quite up to Kyne's expectations, and it appeared the day's total might fall a bit short of his estimate.

But he figured out what to do about that. He would make a big bet on the entry to show, thus increasing the handle, and he would get his money back with a ten percent profit, the minimum a track was required to pay on winning tickets.

Shortly before post time the entry was 1 to 10, and if ever there was a cinch bet on a racetrack, his had to be it. Kyne was not a chalk bettor, preferring longshots, but he bet three thousand dollars to show on the entry. He wanted to make certain he won Solly's bet this time, as Solly had beaten him the last few days. Bill's three thousand dollars was just enough to win his one hundred dollars bet, but all

Frank (Lefty) O'Doul, the baseball star, Gene Normile, who managed Jack Dempsey for a short time, and Joe Cohen and Solly Tichner at Bay Meadows in 1936.

three horses in the McDaniel entry finished out of the money.

Kyne frequently beat the races when he took his betting seriously, but playing the horses at Bay Meadows was a different story. He played for fun more than for profit, and the fun came from having a ticket on the winner. To increase his chances he sometimes bet two or more horses in the same race.

Before coming to the track in the morning he made his own "line," listing the odds he thought each rated. If he didn't like the tote-board odds on his original choice he would play an overlay, a horse whose odds were considerably higher than those on his own line.

During racing seasons Kyne would spend the afternoons

in his Turf Club box, which was easily accessible to friends and acquaintances, and many times a day he was asked for tips.

Quite often Bill's propensity for multiple bets would put him in an embarrassing spot. He would tell a friend the horse he liked, then at the last minute make another bet on Joe Blow because he was an overlay at 15 to 1. It's easy to imagine the friend's chagrin after the race to hear Bill boast that he had bet on the winner—Joe Blow.

One of Kyne's biggest betting thrills came when he was in his twenties and at the races in New Orleans. He had studied the *Racing Form* the night before and had found a long shot he believed would win. The horse was named Bumpsie Ray, and Kyne made a big bet. The horse was far back in the early running, but when the field turned for home, Bumpsie Ray began picking up horses and came charging down the stretch to win by a nose, and Kyne collected close to ten thousand dollars.

In 1932 Kyne and Artie Samish engaged in a torrid golf match in Los Angeles and a betting spree that awed a gallery of friends. (Samish later became a prominent Sacramento lobbyist and during Earl Warren's term as governor got himself in hot water by boasting that he was the behind-the-scene governor of the state.)

Under the headline, "KYNE $5,820 GOLF WINNER" *The San Francisco Examiner* ran the following story on the match:

LOS ANGELES—Nov. 23—(Universal Service) Rancho Golf and Country Club became the Monte Carlo of southern California today when Bill Kyne, former partner of the Tanforan racetrack, and Artie Samish, co-partner of the Baden dog track, engaged in a twosome match which culminated on the seventeenth green with Kyne winning $5,820.

Kyne and Artie Samish, right, at the start of their high-stakes golf match. Frank Flynn (center) was Samish's assistant.

The match was the outcome of a golfing gabfest which began at a downtown hotel in the wee hours of Tuesday morning. It started with Kyne wagering $2,000 that Samish couldn't break 100 and another two grand that Kyne could defeat him in match play. In the Rancho clubhouse an additional wager of $40 a hole was agreed upon as a consolation prize.

Samish lost both bets shooting 105 for eighteen holes and losing two down to Kyne. The additional $1,820 was the outcome of $100 wagers on drives, putts and approaches.

The racing gentry of both species, the horses and dogs, and a gallery of friends, looked on in amazement as the betting was carried from hole to hole.

For years afterward Kyne enjoyed telling about the match, and mentioning that Samish never paid him one dime of the money he won—and he never asked for it.

One of the biggest nonracing bets that Kyne ever won was on the 1939 Rose Bowl game between USC and Notre Dame. USC was a 4 to 1 favorite, and after analyzing the teams' records Bill decided Notre Dame, coached by Knute Rockne, was a big overlay. He collected a whopper of a bet when Notre Dame won.

Poker is another game in which Kyne could more than hold his own, but in the years I knew him, he confined his card playing to social games with close friends.

About once a month a group including Kyne and his wife, the Harold Mundhenks, and Carl De Benedettis, the Mike Naifys, Les Vogel, Jr., and sometimes the George Panarios and Bill Greenbachs would get together for a poker session.

"It was strictly a friendly, social game for fun with a dollar limit," said De Benedetti.

Bill Kyne gambled for fun, excitement, and profit, and no one knows how much he won and lost, but he won the first bet he ever made and he won his last bet—after he died.

His first bet was at the old Emeryville track when he was selling papers there. One day a regular customer bought a paper and then handed him a coin and said, "Here lad, bet this on Molly O in the third race."

"I thought he was kidding," said Kyne. "I thought he had given me a penny, but I took a closer look and it was a five dollar gold piece. Molly O was 20 to 1, and I got a friend to make the bet for me. The horse won and I had the most money I'd ever had in my life."

The genial Irishman didn't live to collect the last bet he made. Shortly before his death he bet on Holandes in the Caliente future book on the Santa Anita Handicap. He placed five hundred dollars to win at 6 to 1 and five hundred dollars to place at 3 to 1. Holandes, one of the horses he had imported from Argentina, ran second, beaten a nose by the lightweighted Corn Husker, who carried 105 pounds while Holandes packed 121. But the bet made a profit of one thousand dollars and Mrs. Kyne collected the winnings.

11

Bill Kyne was responsible for nearly four million dollars being raised for the war effort during World War II.

When the United States entered the war, all racetracks on the West Coast were ordered closed.

In the late summer of 1942 Kyne began negotiations for permission to operate Bay Meadows for the benefit of the war effort. After communicating with various authorities by letter, phone, and a trip to Washington, he received approval from Lt. Gen. John J. De Witt, Western defense commander, William M. Jeffers, rubber administrator, and the California Horse Racing Board—but with many restrictions.

Following are some of the conditions under which the track could conduct races:

Ninety-two percent of all profits to go to the war effort.

Racegoers not permitted to use cars or buses for transportation to the track (due to gas and tire rationing).

The auto parking lots to be closed.

Ten percent of all salaries to be paid in war bonds, and the same for purses to horsemen and jockey fees.

Booths for the sale of war bonds and stamps to be placed at the track.

Only men over forty-five to be employed, except younger

At the beginning of racing for war relief at Bay Meadows the goal was a million dollars. Nearly four million was realized.

men exempt by their draft boards, and women of various ages.

The track to close by 5:00 P.M.

The first of the Bay Meadows war relief meetings, a forty-five-day meeting later extended to fifty-five, opened October 3, 1942. To help alleviate the transportation problem Kyne hired horse-drawn wagons and tallyhos to meet the streetcars that ran from San Francisco to San Mateo and take race fans to the track, about three miles away.

The opening is described by Prescott Sullivan in the following article, reprinted in part from the *San Francisco Examiner*:

Its vast parking area empty of automobiles, the Bay Meadows race track reopened for business yesterday and to the surprise of many doleful prophets, it did pretty well.

Their ingenuity taxed by OPA orders restricting auto and bus travel directly to the track, close to 10,000 persons managed to get there anyhow.

Many of the customers reached the track in a variety of horse drawn vehicles which met street cars at the terminus of No. 40 line to San Mateo. Others, mostly those with A cards* drove their cars to within a discreet distance of the place and walked the rest of the way. A few, posing as commuters, took train and bus to Hillsdale station, which is within a brassie shot of the grandstand, and got off there, although both services had advertised that no race track traffic would be handled.

Arrangements to handle the street car trade were far from perfect. It took us two hours to get from Fifth and Mission Streets to the track. Leaving town at 11:40 we got where we were going just in time to be shut out for the second race which was a good thing because we didn't have the winner.

One hour and ten minutes of this traveling time was spent on the street car, standing up, of course, because the tram, designed to seat about sixty, was loaded with 200.

They were a good natured group, anticipating the fruitful returns of the "hot tips" which all had in abundance. At San Mateo we piled off the car and looked around for one of a dozen assorted horse drawn conveyances the track had promised to have in readiness.

One tallyho, hauled by four mules, and carrying seventy passengers, had left the terminal a few minutes before. Another was fifteen minutes getting to the starting point. Some, impatient to be on their way, walked. Others waited.

Riding one of the wagons was an experience. As the heavy horses plodded through San Mateo streets, dogs intrigued by the strange sight, yapped at their heels. San Mateo residents, standing in their yards, looked on with evident awe. Some shook their heads as if to say "what is the world coming to?" But the merry procession kept rolling. People were going to the races!

On the way back the procession wasn't quite so merry. Race track crowds are never as merry at the end of the day

* Gas-ration cards that allowed the most usage per month.

84

as they are at the start. A guy with whom we had ridden down hadn't cashed a single ticket. He grumbled some.

But another fellow had hit the daily double and he thought everything was swell. He didn't complain at the jostling and delays.

"If I don't get home all night it will be all right with me," he said. "I'm a big winner."

General Manager Kyne promised to have the system going better by tomorrow.

"We'll have more wagons, better drivers and a fellow at the depot to see that things run smoothly."

Only vehicles permitted within the track proper were bicycles and we counted twenty of them. A half dozen saddle horses were tethered close to a watering trough which is new to the Bay Meadows scene.

Our guess is that some of those who saw the possibility of fun and adventure in the tallyho ride to the track will not be so keen about it again. But others will be because, as they say at the club, the true horse player will get to the place where the action is even if has to travel on hands and knees.

Anyway, they's off and running again at Bay Meadows. Get there as best you can.

Bay Meadows conducted meetings in the spring and fall for the duration of the war and was the only track on the West Coast that was permitted to operate.

Here is a sample of some of the checks Kyne issued, though they do not represent the full amount issued to these recipients, which are only a few of about forty that received funds: Army Emergency Relief, $175,000; Western Defense Command, $125,000; Treasure Island Army Base, $56,000; Alameda County War Effort, $82,000; San Mateo County War Effort & Welfare Fund, $104,000; San Francisco County War Effort, $60,000; Stage Door Canteens, $117,000; Livermore Veterans Hospital, $30,000; Marine Corps, $35,000; Hearst War Wounded Fund, $51,000; Navy Hospital, Oakland, $35,000; McClellan Field, $42,000.

One day the commandant at the Mare Island Naval Hos-

Bill Kyne filling in as waiter at the San Mateo Stage Door Canteen.

pital for amputees was a guest at the track and mentioned to Kyne that there was a shortage of artificial limbs and said what the hospital really needed was its own plant to manufacture them. He said he had requested funds from Washington but due to red tape it would be a long time before he got them, if at all.

Kyne told the admiral Bay Meadows would provide the money and he could get started next day. The plant was built, and hundreds of amputees were fitted with limbs long before they would have received them otherwise.

After the war and into the Korean war, Kyne continued to provide funds from Bay Meadows to veterans hospitals, mostly for things not included in their budgets, such as

Wounded service men from Travis Air Force Base on the roof at Bay Meadows. Jack Smith is at right in front row.

Watching the races from the Club House terrace.

Amputees from Mare Island Naval Hospital as guests at Bay Meadows. Jack Smith is at left and Kyne in center.

Luncheon guests of Kyne in the Bay Meadows Club House.

additional television sets, recreation facilities, and sometimes to supplement insufficient budgets. At the Livermore Veterans Hospital a chapel was built with money from the track.

And Kyne furnished the money for many other types of worthwhile projects, including a swimming pool at the Log Cabin Ranch School for delinquent boys at La Honda and fifty thousand dollars for completion of the music auditorium at the College of Notre Dame in nearby Belmont, California.

But money was not all that was provided by the man who had wanted to be a priest.

At the beginning of Bay Meadows' first war-relief season Kyne hired Jack Smith to arrange stage shows for entertainment at veterans hospitals in the area, and to bring groups from the hospitals to the track as guests. Smith was a former racing official and had spent time in an Army hospital overseas during World War I.

He lined up top entertainers who were currently performing in San Francisco stage shows and at hotels and nightclubs. Frequently sports stars were also on his programs.

During one of his war meetings Kyne received a request from an admiral at Mare Island Naval Hospital for a Bay Meadows sponsored show. Bill gave the assignment to Jack Smith.

Jack said, "I learned Maurice Chevalier was going to open at the Curran Theatre in San Francisco in a few days and that he was in New Orleans. I contacted him by phone and asked if he would be a part of our show. He said, 'Mr. Smith, it would be suicide for me to appear before those brave men, because of the bad publicity I received from singing for the Germans when they occupied Paris.'

"I tried to coax him but he said I would have to talk to his manager, who was at the St. Francis Hotel in San Francisco. His manager said definitely 'no.' I told Kyne

I wouldn't give up on him. After he checked in at the St. Francis I got three naval officers to meet me there and we went to his room. He invited us in, and after we calmed his fears, he agreed to accompany us to Mare Island, but said he would sing only one song—and that would be 'Louise.'

"Our show at Mare Island was set for late Sunday afternoon at the hospital theater, and Chevalier's show at the Curran was scheduled for 8:30 that night.

"Besides Chevalier we had Mickey Rooney, the Duncan Sisters, Desi Arnaz, Nat King Cole, and several other stars, but the audience didn't know Maurice was on the program.

"When I announced Maurice Chevalier also was here the audience went wild. Chevalier was so touched he wiped a tear from his eye. Instead of one song, he sang twelve. And he didn't arrive at the Curran until 9 o'clock. When he explained his delay was because he had been entertaining the amputee patients at Mare Island, the audience gave him a standing ovation.

"One day Kyne called me at my home in Los Angeles and asked if I could line up a show for the Travis Air Base Hospital [near San Francisco]. He said he had learned a plane load of wounded was due to arrive soon from Korea and he wanted to provide some entertainment for them, and others at the hospital.

"I told him I could arrange it, so I planned it for a Monday. The commander at the base was enthusiastic because the hospital head always enjoyed and appreciated our efforts. The commander said he would send an army transport plane to pick us up on Monday at 8 A.M. I secured a large group of movie and sports celebrities and told them to report at the airport at 7:30 A.M.

"Don't remember all of them but I had Dan Dailey, Dale Robertson, Chuck Conners, Joe Louis, Mickey Walker, Fidel La Barba, Bob Lemon, some of the Lawrence Welk enter-

The Duncan Sisters entertaining at a Bay Meadows-sponsored veterans' hospital show.

tainers and Trainer Jimmy Jones and Jockey Steve Brooks from the Calumet Stable to talk about Citation, the Triple Crown winner.

"On Sunday, the day before we were to go, I was at a football game at the Coliseum and I was paged over the PA system. I was told the commander at Travis wanted me to call him. When I called he said he couldn't send the plane because all available planes were scheduled for Korea. I was shocked. I had no chance of contacting all of the group and cancelling the trip.

"I called Howard Hughes and all airports and airlines for help, but they couldn't help me, so I went home and prayed. Then I picked up the phone and called the Marine

Base at Camp Pendleton [near San Diego]. I told the sergeant who answered the phone my problem. He said it would be difficult because this was Sunday and all the top brass were off duty, but said not to give up and that he would call me back in an hour.

"When he called back he said a plane would pick us up at 7:30. By 8:30 it hadn't arrived and I called the base and was told the plane was on the runway, but they couldn't release it until they knew who gave the order for the trip. I explained the situation and the man on the line said 'to hell with waiting, the plane will be there in twenty minutes' and it was.

"When we were loaded the pilot told me that if he were ordered to return he would refuse even if it meant a court-martial. When we got to Travis we went to the room where the new arrivals were and I introduced our celebrities. Later we put on a good show at the hall, and it was packed with over one thousand patients."

One day during the war a young lieutenant at the Army base on Angel Island near San Francisco saw a notice inviting military personnel to be the guests of Bay Meadows. This was welcome news to the young officer who was looking for something different to do while waiting to be shipped overseas, and the next day he and a fellow officer went to the track.

They were told to take the elevator to the roof where the manager had special accommodations for military officers and special guests. This was Kyne's private "Penthouse Turf Club," and there were mutuel windows, a free bar, and seats with a good view of the racing strip.

It was there that the lieutenant, tall, lean, and recently out of Harvard, met Bill Kyne, his wife, and daughter, Marylin. He was impressed by the boss's hospitality and his vibrant personality.

It was an important day for the young lieutenant, though he had no way of knowing that one day he would become the president and general manager of the track he was then visiting—and that the attractive young girl he had just met would become his wife. His name? Robert S. Gunderson.

After the races Kyne took Gunderson and the other officer and his wife and daughter out to dinner.

It isn't surprising that Gunderson returned to the track frequently until he was sent to Australia a few weeks later.

Bob Gunderson, Bay Meadows' current manager and president, is a native of St. Paul, Minnesota, the son of a banker of Norwegian stock. He is a graduate of the University of Minnesota and earned a master's degree in business administration at Harvard.

After the end of World War II and his discharge from the Army as a major, he got a job at the Bank of California in San Francisco, and he and Marylin were married.

Bob didn't like working in the bank because he found it too confining, and when Kyne built his Portland Meadows track in Oregon in 1946 Bill persuaded Gunderson to become his operations manager. Kyne knew that his son-in-law—with his education, ability, and his knowledge of business methods—could be an asset to his organization.

When Portland Meadows' season closed Kyne placed Gunderson in charge of the newly opened Bay Meadows Airport, located just north of where the San Mateo County Fair administration building now stands. (Gunderson had a pilot's license.) The purpose of the airport was two-fold: to offer a training course in flying and to be used by owners of private planes on trips to the races. It was a far-sighted idea, but it didn't pay off, and in 1950 the airport was closed and the site was sold to the county fair. Gunderson was then made operations manager at Bay Meadows. He later held the same position at Tanforan and Golden Gate Fields for several years and in 1965 was made general

Robert S. Gunderson, who has been general manager of Bay Meadows since 1969. He also has been president of the California Jockey Club since 1973.

manager of both racing associations. He resigned these positions when he took over the helm at Bay Meadows in 1969.

Kyne received dozens of awards, plaques, citations, and trophies from recipients of his contributions. Here is a sample of the list, with accompanying inscriptions:

U. S. NAVY—Certificate of appreciation for services rendered during World War II.

DISABLED AMERICAN VETS—Distinguished services for exemplary effort for hospital vets.

LOS ANGELES TIMES NATIONAL SPORTS AWARD—For contributions to war relief through racing. (This award was presented to Kyne at a banquet in the Biltmore Hotel in 1943.)

MARE ISLAND NAVAL HOSPITAL—In appreciation for contributions to progress of rehabilitation.

DAMON RUNYON MEMORIAL FUND FOR CANCER RESEARCH—In appreciation for assisting to fight cancer.

MILITARY ORDER OF PURPLE HEART—Award of merit.

91st DIVISION ASSOCIATION—In appreciation of philanthropic acts.

WAR SHIPPING ADMINISTRATION—In appreciation of patriotic contributions made toward the war effort.

FRATERNAL ORDER OF EAGLES—Civic service award.

12th NAVAL DISTRICT—In appreciation of the comfort and welfare of families of Navy, Marine Corps, and Coast Guard.

AMERICAN VETS OF WORLD WAR II—Distinguished services rendered.

U. S. NAVY, BUREAU OF MEDICINE AND SURGERY —Services rendered the Medical Department.

AMERICAN LEGION—In appreciation for meritorious service.

In Ascot Day attire at a recent Bay Meadows meeting are Bob Gunderson, his son, Greg, and daughter, Nancy.

Bill Kyne receiving the Los Angeles Times *National Sports Award for his contribution to war relief, at the Biltmore Hotel in 1943.*

VETERANS OF WORLD WAR II, AMVETS—In recognition of distinguished services rendered.

Kyne received many other honors, including testimonial dinners. I attended a dinner in his honor at the Palace Hotel in 1934 and another at the Fairmont Hotel in 1952, and in going through memorabilia at the home of his daughter I discovered there had been another.

I picked up a menu with Bill's picture on the front cover and the following words:

DINNER
Given In Honor Of
WILLIAM P. KYNE
[His picture]
"Bill"
BLANCO'S
Saturday, March 2, 1918

Bill Kyne was then thirty years old. I have been unable to find anyone who knows why at that age he was honored at a dinner—at one of San Francisco's plush and famous old restaurants, Blanco's.

The menu is interesting. Four different beverages were served during the course of the meal, Gibson cocktail, Cresta Blanca Sauterne Souvenir, Cresta Blanca St. Julien Souvenir, Champagne Paul Masson.

The food course: Fancy hors d'oeuvre, Fresh Crab à la Louis, Chicken Broth with Dumplings, Lobster à la Greque, Chicken Farcie Au Jus, Petits Pois Bonnefemme, New Potatoes Rissole, Cold Asparagus Vinaigrette, Sabaion Frappe, Petits Fours, Roquefort Cheese on Toasted Cracker, Demitasse.

It isn't likely anyone went away hungry.

The dinner at the Fairmont was attended by a sell-out crowd of one thousand, and Kyne was given a new Cadillac. Another award was a commission as a Kentucky Colonel.

DINNER

GIVEN IN HONOR OF

WILLIAM P. KYNE

"BILL"

BLANCO'S
SATURDAY, MARCH 2, 1918

Cover of the menu for the Kyne dinner in 1918.

A distinct Bay Meadows welfare project is the annual Children's Hospital Day Sweepstakes, conducted by the San Francisco Children's Hospital Auxiliary. The auxiliary is composed of a group of women prominent in society, and its purpose is to raise funds for the hospital's building fund. To date the fund has received more than two million dollars from the Bay Meadows sweepstakes project.

In 1937 several of the women met with Kyne and asked for permission to sponsor a hospital day at the races, sell tickets, and keep a percentage of the sales. Kyne said they could, indeed, have a day and the percentage they could keep would be one hundred.

Next day Lanny Leighninger, one of the racing officials, and I were talking and agreed the hospital day would get us some good publicity. Then Lanny said, "You know what would be great, if we could arrange it—get the women to run a sweepstakes. Like the Irish Hospital Sweepstakes."

I said it was a good idea but was doubtful it could be arranged. But we went to Kyne and he liked the idea. He contacted the hospital women and they liked the idea. They said they'd try to get clearance for it, and they did.

They sold tickets for one dollar that were good for admission to the grandstand and a chance for part of twenty-five thousand dollars in prizes, with ten thousand dollars as first prize.

The first race day netted the building fund twenty-eight thousand dollars, and the hospital women were elated. The sweepstakes is now netting over one hundred thousand dollars annually.

12

Kyne usually had two or three people on his payroll simply because they were elderly and had no source of income. One of these was George Busky.

George lived happily, year after year, with his dogs and cats in a stable at Bay Meadows, and though his mode of existence created a fire hazard, all efforts to transfer the old man to better and safer quarters met with the same rebuff.

Each time Kyne would delegate someone to tell George Busky he must move, the message bearer would report back with the same excuse: "Get someone else, I haven't the heart to put him out." And Kyne would nod understandingly. He had been the first to attempt to move the man. One morning several weeks previously he sent for George to come to his office. I was there when Busky arrived. Though he used a cane and arthritis caused him to bend slightly forward from the waist, Busky walked with short, brisk steps across the room to Kyne's desk.

He took a smelly cigar from his mouth and smiled cheerfully as he extended a dirty hand and said, "Good morning, Mr. Kyne, good morning. It's a pleasure to see you this fine morning." There was a hint of an accent, and a quality of dignity in his voice.

Hesitant to come to the point, Kyne asked George how he was getting along. It was the wrong question to ask. Busky assured him things couldn't possibly be better, "Thanks to you, Mr. Kyne, and God bless you." He turned to me and said, "And bless you too, laddie." He usually addressed men as laddie and women as darling or princess, and he was generous with blessings, both his own and those requested from the Almighty.

When Kyne got around to tactfully suggesting that George might be better cared for elsewhere, the old man graciously laughed it off as though he was sure Kyne was not serious. Why, where else could he find such nice people to talk with as Mr. Kyne and the others who worked for Bay Meadows? More important, there were his pets to consider. They would not be pleased with a change.

"I have everything I need," he said.

It was fear of a fire that worried Kyne—and the local fire chief. Busky's poor eyesight, his increasing carelessness, plus his cigar smoking and use of an oil stove for cooking and heating were ample reasons for concern.

Dissatisfied with Kyne's efforts, the fire chief arranged for Busky to move into a cottage behind the home of a widow who would give the old man any needed attention, though the pets would not be accepted.

The chief then gave George an ultimatum, threatened a court order, and said he would return in the morning and help with the moving. Next morning Busky greeted the chief pleasantly, thanked him for his concern, and stated he would not be moving after all. "I had a talk with the Lord last night and He told me He didn't want me to move; that He would not permit a fire. Now a fine man like you wouldn't want to defy the Lord, now would you?"

The chief reported to Kyne: "Busky's got the Lord backing him up. That's too much opposition for me."

George got a twenty-five dollars weekly "pension" from the track, and most of it was used to feed his pets, consisting of three dogs, eight or more cats, a goose, and a duck.

George Busky first came to Bay Meadows in 1940 as a stable hand, though previously he had raced a small stable of his own. At the close of the racing season that year he was left stranded, and Kyne gave him part-time work as a track gardner and permission to occupy one of the stable living quarters.

Though everyone liked George, some said he was a big liar and maybe a mite crazy. Eccentric he was, but crazy he wasn't. It's true, however, that he told conflicting stories concerning his past, of his many adventures and exciting experiences, but George wasn't one to let facts hinder the telling of an entertaining story. Because he told of living in so many different places in the same periods of his life, his actual background was still a mystery when he died in 1956 at an estimated age of eighty. But his story that he was born in Hungary and his father had been associated with a family of royal blood was substantiated by papers found after his death.

The extent of Busky's education wasn't known, but one thing is certain; he was well read and a knowledgeable man on many subjects. He could quote from the classics, as well as from the Bible, and I suspect most of his personal adventure tales came from reading Kipling, Conrad, Wells, and others.

Busky enjoyed pleasing people and never permitted himself to become boring. His keen sense of concern for the attitudes of others was demonstrated at a cocktail party.

The party was in Kyne's spacious office, following the last race on a Saturday. Kyne had invited a group of prominent friends and his staff. He told one of his aides to get clean clothes for Busky and bring him to the affair.

When Busky joined the party some of the guests glanced

at him questioningly, obviously noting his ill-fitting attire and probably thinking he was an intruder. Perhaps it was because the old man sensed this attitude that he made a request to Kyne. They walked to the end of the room and Kyne announced, "I want you people to meet George Busky. He is a good friend and I am glad he could come to our party." Then Kyne astonished the gathering as he said, "George wants to say a prayer."

There was a muffled snicker, a gasp, and I noticed expressions of both sympathy and scorn.

With poise and a crisp, compelling voice, Busky spoke to the gathering. Within seconds there was complete silence and attention.

"First," he began, "I want to tell you that I, a foreigner, consider it a great blessing to be living in such a wonderful country as America. Americans are kind, generous, and friendly. It is right that people should enjoy friendly social gatherings like this, and to be here with you is a privilege for which I am thankful."

Then, with highball in hand, he bowed his head in prayer. Briefly, he thanked the Lord for his good fortune and said he was sure all in the room also were grateful—grateful because they were living in America and could enjoy life and freedom in such a great nation.

For several moments there was silence and, I think, a feeling of humility. Then almost everyone wanted to talk with Busky. After a second drink he declined more. "My motto is, 'If you use liquor don't let liquor use you.' I've learned two drinks are enough for me."

If taking two drinks and smoking foul cigars can be considered vices, then Busky had another. Occasionally he would make a small wager.

His wagers usually were made on advice of a horseman. Before making a bet, George would go to the paddock, watch the horse as it was saddled, then cross himself and head for the mutuel windows. Usually he won, and then his pets enjoyed a feast. Instead of prepared pet food and canned milk he bought sirloin steak and fresh cream. For himself, he bought the ingredients of his usual diet consisting of sandwiches, hamburgers, and hotdogs.

Several times the wife of the track's caretaker, who lived on the grounds, tried supplementing George's diet by taking a warm meal to him, but each time he shared it with his pets.

As he grew older and his sight weaker, he became more dependent upon his favorite pet, an Australian sheep dog named Duchess. Before leaving his quarters he attached a small rope to his belt and the dog's collar, and Duchess served as a guide.

Then Duchess became seriously ill and was placed in a pet hospital. The track's personnel shared Busky's concern. Bulletins on the dog's condition were posted several times daily in the main office and the information relayed to the old man. Everyone was grateful when the dog recovered.

But Duchess also was getting old, and a short time later Busky realized he was no longer able to properly care for himself and his animal dependents. With the assurance that good homes would be found for his pets, Kyne placed him in a home for the aged.

Another Kyne "pensioner" was Bruce Copeland, a former New York sports writer who had a drinking problem. His last job in the East was editor of a weekly racing publication named the *New York Press*. When he lost that job in the late forties he wrote to Kyne for help, explaining he was jobless and broke.

Kyne wired plane fare, and put him on a small salary and told him he could help out in the publicity department. Copeland had once been a good writer, but he wasn't much help in that department. He turned in a story one day

Tom Sharkey, the old-time fighter, was one of Kyne's "pensioners."

showing how much a horse player would have lost if he'd played the favorite in each race at the current meeting and also the loss from betting on the leading jockey. I explained that wasn't quite the type of publicity to induce people to come to the races. Copeland died of a heart attack a few years after Kyne brought him to Bay Meadows.

Tom Sharkey was a "pensioner." Sharkey was a former heavyweight boxer who in his prime fought some of the top title contenders, such men as Bob Fitzsimmons, Jim Jeffrey, Gentleman Jim Corbett.

Sharkey was supposed to be a guard at the mutuel department door, but I never knew of him stopping or questioning anyone who wanted to enter. Much of the time he was away from his post, usually making a bet or cashing a ticket.

13

During 1946 through 1952 Kyne promoted a variety of sports events as a sideline. He liked to keep active during the off-seasons at the track and liked to keep his name in the papers. Several people said he was a publicity hound. To some extent he probably was, but Kyne knew the value of publicity and he regarded even personal publicity as good for any business or promotion he was involved in.

He wanted his name and title on all forms of advertising and printed matter that concerned the track. And it was always to be William P. Kyne and not Bill Kyne. In my news stories while handling publicity for him I always used his full name. But he wanted to be called Bill by casual acquaintances and associates.

While he was visiting a movie studio in Hollywood in the early forties the photo department took a flattering portrait of Kyne that made him look like a movie star, and he wanted it used for publicity purposes for years afterward. He had a huge enlargement made and hung the picture in his office.

Kyne began his extracurricular sports ventures after World War II by promoting a successful benefit golf tournament at Lake Merced in 1949, and for three years starting in 1949 he promoted several boxing matches each year, including two championship bouts.

He matched heavyweight champion Ezzard Charles with Pat Valentine in a title bout at the Cow Palace in San Francisco in 1949, and Charles won by a knockout in the eighth round. He promoted the Sugar Ray Robinson-Bobo Olson middleweight title fight in 1952 in which Robinson retained his title by a decision. Profits from the match went to the Damon Runyon Cancer Fund.

In another Kyne promotion, Joe Louis, who was attempting a comeback in 1951, knocked out Andy Walker in the tenth round. Then Kyne imported a fighter from Argentina named Rafael Iglesias. After a big buildup he was knocked out in the first round of his first match and returned home.

In charge of ticket sales for Kyne's boxing matches was Vi Elliott, now Mrs. Warren Yazzolino. Vi is a fast-talking gal with a quick temper and a salty vocabulary that she learned from some of the people in boxing.

One day Vi got into a heated argument over tickets with Jimmy Murray, who promoted fights in Oakland. Murray, who was an inch shorter than Vi, apparently had never read the book *How to Win Friends and Influence People*, and the argument reached the name-calling stage.

At this point Vi, being involved in the fight game, suddenly decided to become more involved. She doubled up her fist and floored Murray with a right to the jaw.

Murray complained to Kyne, who called Vi into his office.

"Bill Kyne asked me if I did it and I said yes I did, and he said I would have to write a letter of apology. I said I would not! I said, No way. I won't do it, and Bill said, 'then I'll have to fire you.'

"I started crying and Bill said, 'It's all right, I'm not going to fire you,' and then he smiled and said, 'Actually I'd like to have done it myself. But don't you ever do it again.'"

For several years starting in 1950 Kyne promoted the twenty-mile National Championship Motorcycle race at Bay

Auto and motorcycle races at Bay Meadows.

Meadows, and in conjunction with J. C. Agajanian he sponsored auto races, both Indianapolis-type cars and stock cars. Many of the nation's top drivers competed. One of the drivers in the stock-car races was Al Torres, now in charge of the mail department at Bay Meadows.

Also in the early fifties, Kyne and I promoted a series of Saturday night dances in the Bay Meadows Club House. We started off with Dick Jurgens's orchestra and also booked some top local bands, Ray Hacket, Jimmy Diamond, and others, but there were only two occasions when we made any money, and that was on the two dates that we were able to book Harry James. On the afternoon of his first engagement the Bay Area experienced one of its worst rainstorms and it kept up until well into the night. To the surprise of us all we had a full house of one thousand eight hundred.

Movie star Betty Grable accompanied her bandleader husband, and in Kyne's private bar after the dance Harry was still amazed at the turnout and said that when he arrived he was feeling sorry for Kyne and me because of the loss we would take. (We had to give him a substantial guarantee.) When the fellow that was pouring drinks started to give Betty a drink from a bottle of cheap 80-proof bourbon called PM (I don't know how it got there) I told him to pour her a drink from the 100-proof bottle of Harper. But Harry said no, to give her the PM, that the other was too strong. Betty made no comment and accepted the weaker drink. Harry and Betty owned a racing stable and were at the track frequently during racing seasons.

After Harry James played for us the second time, Kyne and I discontinued the dances and ended up about even on the venture.

Kyne tried to get involved in two other sports during the early 1950s. He negotiated for purchase of the San Francisco 49ers and later attempted to buy the Seals in the Pacific

Coast League but was unsuccessful in both deals. Then when it was announced the New York Giants would move to San Francisco and were looking for a site for a stadium, Kyne tried to get them to build in San Mateo. He offered to donate forty acres of Bay Meadows property in back of the stables for a stadium. The only catch was that Bay Meadows would get the concession rights. That way he figured the shareholders in time would be amply paid for the land. Had they accepted he hoped the stadium would be named for him.

14

The man who brought Thoroughbred racing back to California also helped bring Quarter Horse racing back to the American scene.

The Quarter Horse is the original American racehorse. He started life in the early days of the American Colonies and was bred to run a quarter of a mile. George Washington bred and raced the speedy animals.

But by 1830 the racing Quarter Horse had almost been replaced by the imported Thoroughbred. In the early days of the West he was a racehorse second to being a general ranch horse, and raced only in incidental "cow pony" races at rodeos and in match races at ranches.

Then, at the 1949 Bay Meadows Thoroughbred meeting, Kyne scheduled the first race each day for Quarter Horses. That was the first time they had ever raced on a major track, and with pari-mutuel betting.

Following Kyne's introduction of Quarter Horse racing, the larger California fairs conducted two races per day for the short runners.

And it was with Kyne's assistance that Frank Vessels, Sr., built and opened in 1951 the nation's first racetrack for Quarter Horses, at Los Alamitos near Long Beach.

Dr. William J. Ward, who was persuaded by Kyne to become manager of the harness and Quarter Horse races at Bay Meadows.

114

Another "first" in racing was inaugurated at Bay Meadows the following year—a meeting that combined Quarter and harness races on the same program.

Harness races were conducted at the San Mateo track in 1950 and '51 under direction of the Pacific Coast Trotting Association, but they were not profitable and Kyne conceived the idea of the combined meeting. He persuaded a close friend, Dr. William J. Ward, to form a new association known as the California Horse Racing Association for the purpose of conducting the race meetings with five harness and five Quarter Horse races on each day's program. Dr. Ward became the president and general manager.

The meetings were a success from the start, but in 1968, with racing increasing in popularity, it was decided to schedule a separate season for each breed of horses and race the Quarter Horses at night. In May of 1968 the first night racing in California was presented under direction of the newly organized Peninsula Horse Racing Association, with Doctor Ward serving as president and general manager.

In addition to its own racing season and those of the CHRA and the PHRA, Bay Meadows leases its plant to the Tanforan Racing Association for a short fall meeting and to the San Mateo County Fair Association for two weeks of racing in the summer. With nearly two hundred days of racing each year, Bay Meadows is one of the busiest tracks in the nation.

Many "firsts" and innovations were introduced at Bay Meadows—most of them by the track's founder. In addition to presenting the first Quarter Horse and night racing, Bay Meadows was the first track in California to use the total-izator, photo-finish camera, and electric starting gate.

And it was Bill Kyne who arranged for the first race-horse to travel by plane and for the first shipment of a planeload of horses from a foreign country.

The first of these history-making events occurred in Octo-

Bill Kyne on Bart B. S., a Quarter Horse that had set a world record.

El Lobo being loaded for flight to Bay Meadows. Stuart Hamblen is at horse's head. Burl Tatum is to his left in light shirt.

ber of 1945 after Kyne persuaded Stuart Hamblen, a cowboy singing star, to send his stake horse, El Lobo, from Los Angeles to the San Mateo track by plane. A filly named Featherfoot made the trip to keep El Lobo company.

The trip was made in an old Conestoga Flying Tiger cargo plane in which two stalls were built, and it was piloted by Major Bill Hoelle and Captain Bob Sullivan, two former war flyers who had flown over The Hump in Burma.

Also on the flight were two racing officials, George Schilling and Lanny Leighninger, and Burl Tatum, Hamblen's stable manager. Tatum is presently stable superintendent at Bay Meadows.

"The plane was a clumsy, noisy thing," said Tatum, "and when we got here we landed on the Bay Meadows parking

Crowd greets arrival of historic flight, in front of Bay Meadows grandstand.

lot, and taxied up to the grandstand entrance." Asked if he was scared, Tatum replied: "You bet I was. Hamblen didn't make the trip. I think he was scared to."

The plane arrived shortly before noon and was greeted by a battery of newsmen, photographers, newsreel cameramen, and spectators. Kyne celebrated the event by entertaining the press and friends at a luncheon in the Club House.

The season opened next day, and El Lobo, who had been insured for fifty thousand dollars before the trip, ran in the Inaugural Handicap—and won.

In commenting on the historic flight, George Schilling said, "This proves that the day of transporting Thoroughbreds cross-country and from foreign countries is just around the corner, and it will be a boon to major stakes races in the future."

He was right, but it was not until 1956 that Kyne brought eleven horses to Bay Meadows from Argentina, marking the first time a plane full of horses had been flown from one country to another.

Schilling was presiding steward at Bay Meadows and Tijuana for many years, and he is the man who originated the "calling" of a race over a public address system.

It's easy to imagine how unsatisfactory a horse race would be without someone at a loudspeaker describing the positions of horses during the running of a race. Yet, the call of a race over a PA system was unknown to the turf until 1923.

In that year a movie company was making a film at the Tijuana track and part of its equipment was a Magnavox, which the director used to give orders to his crew and cast.

Schilling heard the loud voice and then a sudden thought struck him. Why not borrow the contraption and use it to describe the running of a race for the public? Schilling did and history was made.

Clem McCarthy, Joe Hernandez, and J. J. Murphy got their start as race callers at the Mexican track.

Another Kyne "first" of major importance to the turf was the introduction of the electric, all-enclosed starting gate. It was invented by Clay Puett and used for the first time in America at the Bay Meadows fall meeting of 1939. The electric starting gate has proved one of the most significant innovations in the history of racing, virtually eliminating delays at the post and uneven starts.

In the early days of the turf, dating back to 1668 when organized racing had its inception at Hemstead, New York, starts were effected by lining up the horses in front of a web strip stretched across the track.

This system served fairly well in the beginning, but through the years racing gained in popularity and horsemen began concentrating on breeding faster horses. The race horse became a highly bred, high-strung animal, often fractious and excitable at the starting line. The task of getting the horses off on an even start became more difficult, and long delays upset the track's program schedule.

By the 1920s the problem had become so serious to the steadily growing turf industry that a series of experiments on improved starting methods were begun.

Marshall Cassidy, then a prominent starter, is credited with one of the first innovating starts. At the old Tijuana track he had stationary partitions, open at both ends, installed at the six-furlong and mile-and-a-quarter chutes.

Then in 1924 Puett built a wooden frame starting gate mounted on wheels. He built it in Colorado and used it at fairs in that state.

A few years later two steel-frame portable gates appeared: the Barr gate in the East and the Jarvis gate in the West. They were similar in structure to the gates now in use, but open in front and back.

The next step was to place a padded bar at the back when a horse entered its starting stall. But the horses were unaccustomed to the new contraption and few would stay put.

Jack Jarvis then installed a heavy leather strap across the front of each stall in his gate, with a spring release controlled by the starter. He had the right idea, but his method wasn't practicable. Horses frequently lunged against the strap with their chest, sending their jockeys somersaulting through the air. And too often some of the straps failed to release, trapping one or more horses in the gate. The straps and back bars were soon discarded.

Meanwhile, Clay Puett, a starter and former trainer, had continued his efforts to construct a better gate. He hit the jackpot by installing two wire mesh swinging doors that locked together in a V-shape at the front of each compartment, and a door at the rear to be closed behind a horse. The front wings were released by an electric button in the starter's hand.

If a horse attempted to break through he hit the wire doors with his nose, and once he did that he didn't try it again.

Puett built his gate at Vancouver, Canada, and tested it at the 1939 summer race meeting there. After receiving favorable reports from horsemen, Kyne gave Puett a contract for its use at Bay Meadows. The Puett gate, or gates patterned after it, are now used on all major tracks in North America.

Loans from Kyne helped Puett and Jarvis finance their starting-gate experiments.

Puett and Jarvis were starters for Kyne at Juarez in 1926. Both men asked for the job, and rather than say "no" to one he gave the job to both. One would be the starter one day and the other the next, and on the days when one wasn't the starter he was one of the ground crew, helping line up the horses at the post. It was probably the only time a racetrack had two starters at the same meeting.

"Those two men really detested each other," said Willie Kyne, "and if one got hurt by a horse he got no sympathy from the other."

Previous to invention of the all-enclosed starting gate the turf had several notoriously bad post horses. Among these were McGonigle, The Finn, Chapultepec, Sonny Marcus, Redneck, and a mare aptly named Headache. They were known as rogues or bad actors and sometimes caused delays at the start of up to twenty minutes.

Occasionally it was necessary to blindfold one of these cantankerous steeds to get it in starting position. An assistant starter at the horse's head would yank off the blindfold at the start.

A blindfold was often used on McGonigle, who was

trained by Rusty Brundage, now head clocker at Bay Meadows, and Rusty tells of a remarkable feat by McGonigle that occurred at Caliente:

"I had him entered in the Agua Caliente Cup in 1931, and it was a two-mile race. They had to put a blindfold on him, and the assistant starter missed when he went to pull it off. McGonigle ran the entire race blindfolded—and he finished second. Willie Moran rode him. The race was won by The Choctaw."

Another oddity that brought embarrassment to a starter happened at the old Ingleside Track in San Francisco shortly after the turn of the century.

The fog was so thick one afternoon that spectators could see very little beyond the finish line. As the horses went to the post for a six-furlong race, the jockey on a 50 to 1 shot took his mount to the stretch turn.

The starter failed to notice an absent entrant as he sent the field away, and when the jockey on the turn heard the horses approaching he went into action. The fans were surprised to see the long shot emerge from the fog at mid-stretch and gallop across the finish line fifteen lengths in front. The hoax didn't become widely known until several days later.

Kyne is credited with being the first to install a Finnish steam bath in a track's jockey quarters, following its recommendation by Bing Crosby. After returning from a trip to Europe, Bing told Kyne about the Finnish baths in Helsinki and how great they were. He mentioned they would help jockeys keep their weight down. In those days jockeys bundled up in heavy clothing and did road work to reduce. Modern tracks now have sauna baths for the riders.

And it was Kyne who appointed the first black man to the position of racing official. At Portland Meadows he promoted Walter Carrington from press-box custodian to placing judge.

15

If Bill Kyne had developed an aversion to water it would have been understandable. The flood at Tijuana had cost him fifty thousand dollars. Heavy rains during most of his opening season at Bay Meadows prevented it from being a financial success, and an overflow from the Missouri River once poured into the stable area during a race meeting at Riverside Park in Kansas City. And the fright of his life came when his daughter nearly drowned in the ocean near Del Mar.

But it was at Portland Meadows that water caused his biggest financial disaster.

A week after opening of his 1948 spring meeting the Columbia River went on a rampage, and in the afternoon of Sunday, May 30, a dike on the edge of nearby Vanport broke.

As the water continued pouring through the broken dike it inundated and destroyed the town of Vanport (causing fifteen deaths) and began spilling over onto the racetrack property. Horses were evacuated to high ground near the track. Several men on Kyne's staff, including Ivan Thomas, Bob Gunderson, Charlie Hunter, Bobby Doyle, and Charlie Dougherty, helped with the evacuation.

Kyne didn't reach the scene until next morning, and by

then Portland Meadows was under thirty-three feet of water. Dougherty, one of Kyne's racing officials, tells of Kyne's reaction:

"Kyne and I and several others were standing on high ground watching the Columbia River flood the track, and my thoughts were on the loss of my weekly paycheck, but standing next to me was a man who was viewing the loss of a fortune, and his first comment was, 'Don't worry, there will always be ham and eggs.' Then he said, 'Let's all go have a drink.'"

You have to take the bitter with the sweet.

As Dougherty's thoughts dwelled on the man who had given him his start in racing he remark: "It was Bill Kyne's optimistic outlook, made of courage and kindness, that won him the acclaim and friendship of thousands of people."

Kyne had only been joking when he mentioned going for a drink—at least right then. Instead, he went to where the horsemen and horses were and began looking after their welfare.

His secretary, Mae De Vol, tells how he handled the situation:

"Mr. Kyne instructed Charlie Hunter and me and two or three others on his staff to set up an emergency office, and we used an old van. We had the use of a motorboat called an Army Duck. (It was loaned to Kyne by Ben Gilmore, head of the Portland branch of the Gilmore Steel Company.) From the boat we were able to step through a window of the Club House's second floor and get a table and some chairs.

"The previous afternoon we had moved important records and papers from the ground-floor office to the Club House. Fortunately the water didn't quite reach the Club House floor, but it came within inches of it.

"When we got the office set up in the van, Kyne sent out for food, cold cuts and other types of food, and said

124

Portland Meadows in the early stages of the flood.

everyone was to be fed. And if anyone wanted a highball he had that for him too."

Kyne's faith in his fellow man is well exemplified by an act that Mae described as she continued:

"Then he gave me a lot of bills—tens, twenties, fifties, and hundreds—I don't know how much—and said every horseman who asked for it was to be given money and no names were to be taken and no record of the amounts. When I ran low on money he gave me more. Most of those I gave money to had gone to Kyne first and he sent them to me. He said they would pay it back, and they did. I know of one man who took two years, but he came in and gave me fifty dollars."

Frequently at the end of Kyne's race meetings he had loaned money to horsemen who needed it to get to the next track, but he had kept a record, and he usually got it back.

Most of the stranded Portland Meadows horses were moved temporarily to a nearby ranch, and then to other tracks.

Kyne rebuilt the Oregon track, and shortly after his death his widow sold it, but got back only part of the fortune that had been lost.

One of the many adversities that Kyne experienced occurred in the last year of his life. He and Joe Cohen owned the Universal Totalizator Company, a small firm whose equipment was used at county fairs and for selling daily-double tickets at Bay Meadows. (The American Tote did not originally have daily-double facilities.)

At the 1956 spring harness races at Bay Meadows the Universal Tote goofed and overpaid winning double tickets. The payoff, as later discovered, should have been $28.00. But the malfunctioning tote said to pay $269.70, and that's what was paid to each winning ticket holder. The overpayment amounted to $79,831. It was the largest overpayment of this type in racing history.

The tote company was responsible for the error, and Kyne announced that he and Cohen would personally pay the deficit.

"This is a jolt," said Kyne, "but I'm used to bad breaks and I've learned that crying for yourself never does any good." *You have to take the bitter with the sweet.*

Another payment Kyne made from his pocket—though not as much—was when he paid off an outdated ticket. Kyne received a letter and a two-year-old two dollar mutuel ticket from Fall River, Massachusetts, with a request for payment. The sender said he had bet on a winner in 1942, when he was in the Navy, and intended to collect next day but was shipped to the South Pacific. The state racing law decrees if a ticket isn't cashed within sixty days after close of a meeting it is invalid, and the state gets the money. But Bill contended a winning ticket should be good as long as a track operates. After records showed the sailor's ticket was on a winner that paid forty-two dollars, Kyne sent him a personal check. He concluded his letter to the sailor in typical Kyne fashion: "If you are out this way again look me up. If you need a job I'll have one for you."

Kyne wasn't old-fashioned, but he did use several outdated phrases in his letters, and when he enclosed a check he always wrote, "enclosed please find. . . ."

16

Kyne made friends with people in all strata of life and was at ease with celebrities, statesmen, and royalty.

Once his guests in the Bay Meadows Turf Club were Saudi Arabian Prince Faisal (who later became king and was assassinated) and his younger brother, Prince Khalid, now king. After their visit Kyne boasted in a jocular vein that now if he needed a loan he knew where to get it.

When Pierre Monteux, conductor of the San Francisco Symphony Orchestra, announced in 1952 that he was retiring, Kyne sponsored a gala farewell dinner for the noted musician. It was a benefit affair, held in the Bay Meadows Turf Club, and supported by the San Francisco Musical Association and The College of Notre Dame. Nearly three hundred people attended, and proceeds went to help build the auditorium on the Notre Dame campus at the neighboring town of Belmont. It was through additional efforts of Kyne that most of the funds for the auditorium were raised.

Many people prominent in the movie industry became racing fans after Santa Anita opened, and Bay Meadows received a sizable share of their patronage.

Saudi Arabian Prince Faisal, left, and Prince Khalid, as guests of Kyne.

At one race meeting Bing Crosby spent a two-week vacation at the track that Kyne built. He and his wife, Dixie, were house guests of Lin and Anita Howard, and the two men were at the track each day of the two weeks. Bing had a box in the Club House and went into the more exclusive Turf Club only once, just for a look.

The following year Bing and Lin, the son of Charles S. Howard, who owned Seabiscuit, formed the Binglin Stable, bought some good horses, and won several stake races.

Another Hollywood celebrity who became a stable owner was Louis B. Mayer, head of the Metro-Goldwyn-Mayer Studio. His first stake-race victory came when Manners Man triumphed in a handicap race at Bay Meadows.

Mayer's tyrannical qualities were well known to the movie industry, but I can truthfully say I am one of the few people

At the farewell dinner in Bay Meadows Turf Club for retiring San Francisco Symphony Orchestra conductor Pierre Monteux, at the mike.

who ever put the man in his place. When Manners Man won I rushed the owner to the winner's circle to receive a trophy and pose for the track photographer. I explained that when the horse came into the winner's circle his place for the picture was at the horse's head. But Mayer was as excited as a child with a coveted new toy and kept shaking the hands of those offering congratulations. The jockey, horse, and photographer were waiting, and after he ignored my request to stand in front of the horse I took the movie mogul by the arm and guided him to *his place*.

Kyne made friends with animals as well as people, and one of his animal friends was a golden cocker spaniel named

Louis B. Mayer, Kyne, and Ben Swig, owner of San Francisco's Fairmont Hotel.

Tippy whose owners lived close to the track and were away from home during the day.

One summer the lonesome canine wandered over to Bay Meadows and became a daily visitor in the business offices, where she made new friends.

When the opening of the fall racing season approached, the office staff was concerned over Tippy being halted at the gates, but Bill came up with a solution. He had a pass printed for Tippy and it was attached to her collar. It read:

SPECIAL PASS
(Tax exempt. Good at all gates)
B A Y   M E A D O W S
Issued to: Tippy
A loyal friend of Bay Meadows
Signed:　Wm. P. Kyne
　　　　　General Manager

Bill Kyne's captivating personality, his infectious smile that was frequently accompanied by a twinkle or sparkle in his Irish blue eyes, made him attractive to women. Recently one of the girls in the Bay Meadows office, Rusty Mathieson, who had never known the man, was looking at a portrait of Kyne on the wall and remarked, "It's his eyes that impressed me most when I first saw the picture. You can see a sparkle that tells you he was a kind, pleasant person."

One of Kyne's feminine admirers in the early fifties was Peaches Browning, a buxom blond with plump legs. Some twenty years previously Peaches had been involved in a sensational scandal in New York that made headlines across the nation, caused by her relationship with millionaire industrialist Edward Browning, who had a yen for teenage girls and became known as Daddy Browning.

Browning entertained young girls with lavish parties in his home, and Peaches became his favorite. The young girl's widowed mother encouraged the friendship. Peaches was fourteen and Browning was fifty-four. But when Browning applied to the court to adopt Peaches there was a howl from the public and the adoption was denied. Then Daddy Browning married Peaches. The marriage didn't last long, and after a sensational divorce trial in which Peaches went into details regarding their sex relations, she was granted a divorce and a substantial cash settlement. Later she and her mother moved to Atherton, near Bay Meadows.

Frequently Peaches was at the Villa Restaurant bar when Kyne came in for lunch, and the amiable Irishman was amused by her flirtations. He gave her passes to the races, though Mrs. Kyne didn't approve of "that woman" being in the Turf Club.

Though Bill never gave his wife the slightest reason for concern, Dorothy was aware of his popularity with women and she was inclined to keep an eye on him.

Once when Peaches and Kyne were engaged in a tête-à-tête at the Villa bar, Solly Tichner, who never missed a chance to pull a joke on his boss, turned toward the door and in a loud voice said, "Hello, Mrs. Kyne." Bill jerked around so fast he spilled some of his drink.

Kyne's popularity with the press resulted in a great amount of publicity, both personal and for his business. Though he never bragged and only talked about himself when answering questions, he did, however, want and seek publicity for his philanthropies.

Sometimes a sports writer would criticize or write something uncomplimentary about Kyne's management of the track, but Bill ignored it and remained as friendly to the writer as if he had never read it. And he never corrected a writer for an incorrect statement.

For this reason several fallacies concerning Kyne and his activities in racing have persisted through the years. One is that Pancho Villa, the Mexican revolutionist, shot a cannonball through a steeple on the Juarez grandstand when Bill was managing the track in 1926. Villa was ambushed and slain in 1923.

133

It's true there was a hole in the steeple when Kyne was at the Mexican track, but it was put there years previously during a battle between Villa's forces and his enemies, at a time when there was no racing.

Then it has been incorrectly stated that Kyne turned down an opportunity to build a track in Southern California, preferring the San Francisco area. From the time he began working to legalize racing he had wanted to build his track in or near Los Angeles.

Another inaccuracy is the belief of many that Bill Hornblower and Joe Cohen were Kyne's partners in his campaigns for the return of racing and in the establishment of Bay Meadows. Hornblower first came into the picture after defeat of the first racing measure, when Kyne persuaded him and Tom Maloney to introduce a racing bill in the state legislature, and Bay Meadows had been operating for several years before Cohen even became a member of the board of directors. Neither had an office at the track while Kyne was manager. Cohen, however, was a substantial investor when the track was first built. But Kyne at no time had a partner in his operation of Bay Meadows. As Sports Editor Curley Grieve aptly put it: "Kyne was Bay Meadows and Bay Meadows was Kyne."

Kyne probably wouldn't have had a board of directors if the law hadn't required it. He ran Bay Meadows as though he were the sole owner. He would listen to occasional advice and complaints from directors, and then do as he pleased.

One of Kyne's directors in the early years of the track was George Marshall, a man who approved of taking money in but not in paying it out.

One season business was below expectations and Marshall kept telling Kyne to cut down on expenses. Then one day Marshall went to the press box and said, "I just read the riot act to Bill Kyne about expenses around here and I told him he had to cut the purse for the San Jose Handicap [the next stake race] from $15,000 to $10,000."

After Kyne heard what Marshall had said to the press, he told me to write a news release. This is the way it started: "William P. Kyne, general manager of Bay Meadows, today announced the purse for the San Jose Handicap has been increased from $15,000 to $20,000."

Of Kyne's many turf-writer friends who covered the races during his years at Bay Meadows only two are still on the job as this book is being written. They are Jack Menges of the *Oakland Tribune* and Ed Romero of the *San Francisco Examiner*.

"Bill Kyne was one of the kindest, most generous men I've ever known," said Romero. "Twice I asked him if he could give a friend of mine a job and both times he said 'yes' and he did."

17

At one Bay Meadows winter meeting an episode occurred that could be entitled "The Mystery of the Seventh Goose."

There were two ponds in the track's infield before it was converted into a golf course, and they were the habitat of domestic geese, ducks, and a few swans. Joe Cohen, the track's assistant manager, took a special interest in them and at times personally fed them. When one of the flocks became overpopulated Cohen gave some of the fowl away.

A few days before one Christmas Joe asked each member of the office staff and maintenance crew to take a goose for Christmas dinner. (I don't mean the goose was to be a dinner guest.) Ralph Barnes, the track superintendent, who was in charge of feeding the fowl, caught the geese and handed out most of them live. He thinned the flock down to six.

Some of those who accepted a goose said theirs was tough and some got young, tender ones. Mae De Vol had invited dinner guests, but never could get her goose tender enough to eat. She and her guests went out to dinner.

I never did learn whether the one I took home was tender or tough. I put him in our enclosed backyard, and my wife and nine-year-old son found him quite sociable. They named

Joe Cohen, who served as Bay Meadows' general manager and president from 1959 to 1969.

him Alexander Swoose, and three days later when it came time to prepare him for the oven, they protested, "We can't eat Alexander!" and we didn't. Next evening at dusk we put him in the car and sneaked him back where he came from. Ralph Barnes was puzzled by the appearance of an extra goose, and if he reads this it will clear up the mystery of how that seventh goose got there.

Another goose story with a Bay Meadows connection is the one about Goglin's goose, who, it seemed, could foretell the winner of a race. A. J. Goglin, a horse owner and trainer, gained possession of Granny, a goose of unknown breed and mysterious origin, in an unusual manner.

He was racing his small string of Thoroughbreds at the county fair at Santa Rosa in the summer of 1965.

"One morning I saw a man at the end of my stable holding a string tied to a goose's leg, and the leg was rubbed raw," Goglin said.

"When I told the man that was no way to treat a goose he just looked at me for a minute. Then he handed me the string and said, 'Here, you can have her,' and he walked away.

"Funny thing; I know just about everybody in the stable area but I'd never seen that guy before—and haven't seen him since," commented Goglin. (Visitors are not allowed in stable enclosures at California tracks, except with special permission.)

After Goglin treated and bandaged the goose's injury she accepted his feed stall as her sleeping quarters.

Next morning she wandered around the stables and then spent several hours in the stall of Mighty Regal, a Goglin-trained horse to race that afternoon. He won easily, paying $5.20 on a $2.00 pari-mutuel wager.

Two weeks later Goglin moved to the San Mateo County Fair and shortly Granny made a lengthy morning visit with King's Currency on the day he was scheduled to race. King's Currency also won, and paid $6.00.

After another two-week lapse, Granny, now at the fair in Stockton, spent the morning with Necessary. The horse won his afternoon race for a $7.20 payoff.

Goglin now took note that three times his goose had spent several hours with a horse, that each time the horse was to race that day, that each time the horse had won.

"It did strike me as kind of strange," Goglin said. "But I figured it was just a coincidence. All three horses were short odds so their winning wasn't any big upset."

Once again Granny waited two weeks, and then made a change in the pattern of her "victory visits" that startled her owner.

Three times within eight days she visited a horse. As before, the horse was scheduled to race that afternoon. But this time none of the horses was a favorite.

On September 10, at Sacramento, the goose paid a repeat visit with Necessary. Though racing against stronger competition, Necessary was first across the finish line, and this time paid $27.40.

By now Goglin could no longer pass off the strange behavior of his pet as mere coincidence.

"It was still hard for me to believe she was psychic or that sort of thing, but she sure did make me wonder."

Goglin seldom bet on a horse, but when Granny's next "tip" came one week later, September 17 (he was now back at Bay Meadows), he made a modest wager. That morning his goose called on Harbormaster, and Harbormaster's afternoon victory returned $16.80 for $2.00.

Early next morning, Goglin was surprised and delighted to see Granny stroll into the stall of Necessary, scheduled to race again that afternoon.

For the sixth straight time, Granny's charm paid off. Necessary's winning effort rewarded his backers, including Goglin, with a $15.40 payoff.

Goglin now was convinced. He couldn't explain it but his goose had proved she could accurately foretell the win-

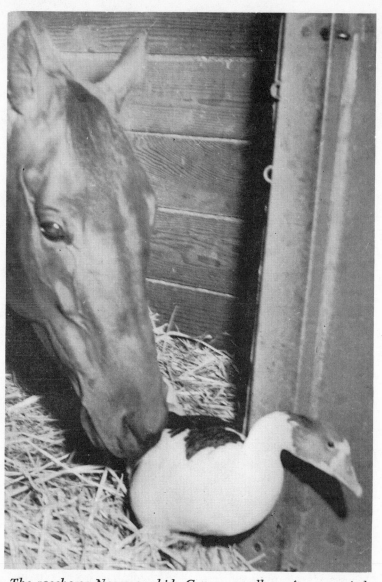

The racehorse Necessary bids Granny goodbye after one of the goose's victory visits.

ner of a horse race. Not once had she visited a horse that hadn't won. Her visits had become more frequent and the payoffs more lucrative.

Horse players dream of situations like this—but this was no dream. Goglin thought of the fortune that soon would be his.

By now though, Granny's phenomenal gift had become the talk of the stable area and she received the attention of a celebrity.

She was visited, watched, and followed constantly. Stable hands, hoping to cash a bet, shooed her into stalls, and tried forcing her visits—unsuccessfully.

Perhaps it was this disconcerting annoyance that caused Granny to change her behavior. Or perhaps, as with the legendary goose that laid the golden egg, it was greed.

But whatever the cause, Goglin's strange goose ceased her visits. Shortly afterward she mysteriously disappeared.

"Maybe," commented Goglin, "she figured she had repaid me for my kindness.'

Wistfully he added, "If I'd only known. I've figured up that if I had started with only $20.00 and bet the winnings back each time I would have wound up with $452,000."

An oddity of a different type concerns the man who was Bay Meadows' head bookkeeper for thirty-one years, Dale Wolfe. When Dale came to the track in 1945 he had never seen a horse race. When he died in 1976 he still had not seen a race. Dale could easily have walked a few yards from his office to the front of the Club House and watched a race, but he never did.

It's a good thing for racing that all people don't have the same attitude toward the sport that Dale Wolfe had.

But an oddity that's difficult to top is the one concerning former Jockey Ralph Neves. Ralph was involved in a spill during a race at Bay Meadows in the 1940s and was taken unconscious by ambulance to Mills Hospital. On arrival he was pronounced dead.

A few minutes later he startled a nurse by getting to his feet and announcing he had to get back to the track to ride in the next race. Before he could be stopped, he rushed out the front door and took a taxi to the track. Next day he resumed riding.

18

Kyne seldom got perturbed when things didn't go as planned. He wasn't upset when one of his St. Patrick's Day luncheons didn't go according to schedule.

Among nearly three hundred guests at the corned beef and cabbage luncheon in the Bay Meadows Club House were members of the California Horse Racing Board, who were guests of honor, politicians, city officials, the press, racing officials, horse owners, and trainers. Guests were given shamrocks and green Irish hats made of cardboard.

On one page of the green menu was listed the luncheon program:

Toastmaster: George Murphy
Introduction of guests
Welcome: William Patrick Kyne
Entertainment: George Murphy, Michael Brennan,
              The Duncan Sisters, Charlie Sims

Sims played the accordion and was to accompany George Murphy, a former vaudeville star and one of Kyne's top officials, and the other singers. The retired Duncan Sisters, as Topsy and Eva, had been famous stage stars for years. Brennan was a good-natured Irishman with a fine tenor voice.

One of Kyne's St. Patrick's Day lunches in the Bay Meadows Club House.

The mike for the entertainers was near one end of the head table, and when the Duncan Sisters walked in they spotted it and began singing. After they had sung song after song, George Murphy walked over as they finished a number and politely told them there were others on the program and to please take a break.

"No, no, go away, we're not through yet," said one of the sisters, and they rushed into another number.

The guests sipped their wine and began their salads and the former troupers sang on and on. When the guests no longer bothered to applaud, Topsy and Eva requested encores from each other. Murphy again approached the pair and again was shooed away. Then when they ran out of songs they began singing the same ones over again. Apparently they wanted to make up for the years they had been out of action.

When the guests finished their dessert some went to the free bar and some began to leave—and the Duncan Sisters sang.

Kyne was merely amused. All had enjoyed a good lunch. Maybe all but George Murphy and Mike Brennan, who never did get to sing their Irish songs.

Some of Kyne's business methods could well be termed unconventional. At least that was the opinion of the manager of the bank that had the Bay Meadows account.

When Kyne applied for a fifty thousand dollar loan to the track the bank manager asked why he wanted it. Kyne said it was to pay dividends. The banker said that was no way to run a business; that dividends should come from profits. Kyne replied that the track was his business and that he would run it the way he wanted; that Bay Meadows had good credit, no debts, and was worth five million dollars—sufficient collateral—and that if his bank didn't want to grant the loan he would get it elsewhere. He got the loan. He repaid it when due a year later from profits of the next meeting, which also produced enough revenue to pay a dividend for that year.

Kyne received some criticism from his directors for his lenient pass policy (one year he sent passes to everyone in the San Mateo County phone book) and for his refusal to charge a parking fee the first few years the track operated. Other tracks had a tight pass policy and charged for parking.

Yet Bay Meadows has paid a dividend every year except when it ran for war relief and for 1949, when $1,700,000 was spent for improvements of the plant. Bill had originally planned to spend $250,000 but kept finding more improvements to be made. The first year the track made no money, but Kyne paid a $10.00 per share dividend with outstanding preferred stock.

After the first four years shareholders had received one hundred percent return on their investments.

One of Bill Kyne's unorthodox transactions resulted in considerable adverse publicity.

All tracks in California are required by the state to have charity days with all profits going to deserving causes, the number of days depending on the length of the meeting. Bay Meadows had five, and Kyne had sole say as to disbursement of the funds.

In 1952 the state's attorney general, Edmund G. (Pat) Brown, who later became governor, launched an investigation of racing's charity funds, starting with Bay Meadows. Local newspapers ran the story on the front page, one under a headline reading: "Kyne's Handling of Charity Funds Under Investigation."

Brown later stated that in conducting the probe he was not looking for, nor did he expect to find, any dishonesty, but that he wanted to determine whether the funds were being allocated impartially and properly.

Perhaps Kyne's reputation for being reluctant to say "no" had some bearing on the probe being ordered.

To Bill Kyne money was merely something to exchange for something needed or wanted or to be used for the benefit of others. When someone needed money Kyne was the man to see. When he needed it himself he borrowed it. And he *always paid it back*.

So he thought nothing of taking some of the idle money in the charity account as a temporary loan when he needed some immediate cash for his Portland track.

When the investigation was announced, the *San Francisco Chronicle* assigned an investigative reporter named Hale Champion to the case. (Champion later became executive secretary to Gov. Pat Brown and after Jimmy Carter became President he was appointed undersecretary of the Health, Education, and Welfare Department.)

Champion began making frequent trips to the track for information. Kyne treated him in his usual friendly manner and answered all questions frankly, though the reporter's stories were not exactly favorable to Kyne.

Attorney Hornblower protested: "Don't tell those reporters anything, don't show them anything; don't even talk to them."

But when Champion asked if he could see the records, Kyne said, "Certainly," and he showed the newsman where they were kept. He provided a desk and chair and said, "You can check all the books and records you want to; I have nothing to hide."

It was with surprise that Champion found something many people might consider something to hide. It was the record of a check for fifty thousand dollars payable to Portland Meadows and drawn on the charity fund account.

The newspapers played this for all it was worth. It was bad publicity for Kyne and for Bay Meadows—a new experience for the amiable Celt who had received so much favorable and laudatory publicity.

Bill Kyne had taken bitter disappointments and financial losses without it affecting his pleasant disposition and ready smile. But this was different. It was a slur on his reputation, his integrity, and it hurt him deeply.

Bill's secretary, Mae, commented recently: "Mr. Kyne just didn't consider he had done anything wrong. He felt he was largely responsible for the money being there in the first place and that it wasn't being used or needed for a while, and of course it was to be returned. He was proud of the money raised for charity through his efforts."

After a definite commitment from Kyne for repayment of the loan and a stipulation from the attorney general's office that henceforth all racing charity funds would be allocated by an impartial committee composed of business and professional men, the investigation was closed.

19

Kyne's desire to please people sometimes went to extremes. On his large desk was a silver-plated statue of a horse, an appropriate and attractive ornament admired by many. One day George McQueen, a local newspaperman, and his ten-year-old daughter Gloria were in Bill's office and Gloria kept admiring the horse, commenting on its beauty.

"Would you like to have it?" Kyne asked.

"Oh, yes," beamed the young lass. Her astonished father made some protesting remark that it was too valuable and she shouldn't accept it, but Bill picked up the statue, handed it to her and said, "Here, it's yours." I was annoyed at the boss for giving it away.

On another occasion Kyne gave away a real horse to a young girl—a racehorse named William K., after himself.

At one of the Bay Meadows meetings a mare surprised her owner by giving birth to a colt in her stall. At the end of the meeting the owner moved on, abandoning the mare and foal. George Busky discovered them and began taking care of them. The owner couldn't be located, and after the foal was weaned a home was found for the aged mare, a cheap plater who could no longer win races, but Busky persuaded Kyne to let him keep the colt, contending he was a future Kentucky Derby winner.

For two years Kyne paid the feed bills, and when the animal reached racing age he obtained registration and ownership papers and turned the colt over to a trainer to be prepared for a turf career. Busky gave him his name.

William K. began his career at the county fair in Vallejo and became one of the most consistent horses on the fair circuit. He always finished last. Well, once he did finish next to last when another horse went lame. After seven starts Kyne gave up on him as a racehorse.

Under the heading of "How Nancy Got Kyne's Horse," sports writer Will Connolly wrote the following article in the *San Francisco Chronicle*:

> You could write anecdotes until knigdom come about Bill Kyne, the race track man. Many of them are for laughs but this one is on the tender side. It is about a high school girl from Larkspur named Nancy who is now in junior college. The young lady has the distinction of owning the only race horse named for William P. Kyne. Bill himself gave her the chestnut colt and signed over registration papers.
>
> Nancy was 15, going on 16, when she first met Bill Kyne. She was a precocious equestrienne from grammar school days. She used to earn spending money by exercising horses at a Fairfax stable after school hours and during summer vacation.
>
> Like Kyne, she enjoyed being around horses. She pestered the stable master to let her curry and comb the animals. Soon as she was old enough to wear blue jeans and her father's shirt, the man allowed her to fork hay and ride rented horses.
>
> We happened to know Nancy from her birth, and, knowing her affection for horses, arranged a meeting with Kyne. She was up on Cloud Eight, and couldn't have been more impressed had we fixed an audience with the President in the White House.
>
> Kyne was equal to the occasion, as he always was. He gave Nancy the grand tour of Bay Meadows and bought her lunch in the Turf Club. The only thing wrong, ol' Bill kept

calling her "little girl." This nettled Nancy, for she was wearing high heels and in two months would be sixteen.

"Tell you what, little girl, I have a horse for you," Kyne said. "But first I want to be sure you can handle him. Let's you and I get in the car and drive to the barn area."

Kyne was genuinely solicitous about turning over a race horse to a teenager, especially a girl. The tall beasties are schooled to be aggressive and are not often easily handled by amateurs. They aren't gentle riding academy plugs.

Nancy dismissed Kyne's fears by walking into the stall and stroking the thoroughbred on the neck and rump with a firm hand. The horse reacted kindly to her hands.

"He's yours," Kyne said. "Take him home."

William K. was a bit too slow to win on a race track. Kyne could have sold him to a farm for several hundred dollars. Instead, he gave him away for nothing to Nancy.

Not only that, but Bill paid for vanning the colt across the Golden Gate Bridge to Fairfax, so Nancy could ride her William K. over Tamalpais trails.

Nancy changed the formal William K. to "Bill," and nothing could have pleased Bill Kyne more. They exchanged Christmas cards thereafter.

It has often been said that Bill Kyne didn't know how to say "no," especially when asked for money. One day Bill and Abe Kemp, the *Examiner* turf writer, were standing in the Turf Club talking when a well-dressed black man walked up and said, "Mr. Kyne, will you loan me a hundred dollars for a few days?"

Kyne pulled out his bankroll and peeled off a one hundred dollar bill. When the borrower walked away Kyne asked Abe, "Who was that man?"

Abe said, "I thought you knew him. That's Johnny Davidson. He's a clocker. You'll get your money back."

Next day Davidson returned the hundred.

While Kyne didn't like to say "no," there were times when he seemingly didn't know how to accept a "no" from others.

George Zarelli can attest to that. George had returned to his home in Millbrae (near San Francisco) at the conclusion of Del Mar's 1947 meeting where he was a patrol judge. He received a call from Kyne in Portland where Kyne had finished building Portland Meadows. Zarelli says this is the way the conversation went:

KYNE: George, I want you to come up here and take the job as racing secretary.

ZARELLI: I can't do it, Mr. Kyne, I'm leaving on vacation in two days.

KYNE: I'll have tickets for you and your wife at the San Francisco Airport tomorrow.

ZARELLI: But, Mr. Kyne, we're going on vacation. I've made all the arrangements.

KYNE: That's fine, George, I'll have a man to pick you up here at the airport.

ZARELLI: I can't make it, we're going. . . .

KYNE: That's fine, I'll see you Thursday. (End of conversation.)

And that's how George Zarelli became racing secretary at Portland Meadows.

Early in the 1950s Kyne offered Zarelli the job of racing secretary at Bay Meadows.

"I told Bill no, that I didn't want the job. I heard nothing more about it until two weeks later when I was on vacation in Victoria, Canada, and received a phone call from George Schilling [Kyne's presiding steward]. Schilling said he had called to congratulate me on my new position as racing secretary at Bay Meadows.

"When I recovered from my surprise I told Schilling there must be some mistake, that I had turned the job down. Schilling said, 'No, there's no mistake, I have the list of officials here and it's been approved by the racing board and published in the press.'"

And that's how George Zarelli landed the job of racing secretary at Bay Meadows.

George was once convinced, for a short time, that Kyne actually could say "no." About midway during the 1956 meeting Zarelli went to Kyne's office and told Bill that because the track was having a record season he thought the racing secretary was entitled to a raise.

Kyne said, "You knew what you were getting at the start of the meeting, didn't you?"

"Yes," replied Zarelli.

"Well, that's what you'll get." After a pause Kyne asked, "How much of a raise did you have in mind?"

George said, "I told him but he didn't say anything. Then when the meeting was over I got a raise for the entire meeting—for double the amount I told Kyne I had wanted."

Another employee who couldn't get the Bay Meadows boss to accept "no" as an answer was June Pierce. June, an attractive girl with a pleasant personality, was a Turf Club usherette. When Kyne installed an elevator to the roof press box and his Top of The Meadows in the forties he told June she would be the operator.

"I didn't know anything about running an elevator and I told Mr. Kyne I didn't want that job. He said, 'June, that's a good job and you will like it and I want you to take it.'"

June has been the elevator girl ever since and she does like the job.

Giving jobs to people who didn't ask for them was not unusual for Bill Kyne. In January of 1943 he was in Mills Hospital recovering from an auto accident in which he and Mrs. Kyne were injured while riding with another couple. Their car was hit by another driven by a young man.

Kyne had a private nurse named Grace Gerken. She said, "He was a good patient and a lot of fun and I would kid him. One day he said, 'How would you like to be a nurse at Bay Meadows?' I said, 'a n-u-r-s-e? at a *racetrack*?' I'd never heard of such a thing. [She didn't know racetracks had an emergency hospital with a doctor and nurse on duty.]

Mr. Kyne laughed, and I said what would I do? He said the nurse that was there got married and wouldn't be back and the job is yours. And I said I would have to think that one over, but he insisted and I said I'd try it."

Grace tried it, liked it, and stayed until she retired in 1974.

As with Grace Gerken, Kyne usually became friendly with an employee of any firm who was frequently of service to him and then he would want to hire the person.

It was because of this trait that he was able to hire O. Henry. On his frequent trips to Portland when he was building his track there he traveled by train and became acquainted with a dining room waiter, a pleasant and likable black man named O. Henry. He persuaded Henry to become his headwaiter in the Portland Meadows Club House, a position he's held for thirty-two years.

Ralph Cunningham is another who was given a job without asking for it. He was in the Navy, a chauffeur for Admiral Greenslade, who was commandant of the 12th Naval District in San Francisco. His job was also to chauffeur visiting officers of high rank and at times drive cars for Admirals Halsey, Nimitz, Osterhaus, and King.

One day in 1947 he drove Admiral Osterhaus to Bay Meadows where he was Kyne's guest, and Ralph accompanied him to the Top of The Meadows. When Osterhaus casually mentioned that Ralph would get his discharge in a few weeks Kyne said, "Tell him to come see me, I'll give him a job." Cunningham became Bill's regular driver and was also assigned some office work.

During one of the Portland Meadows meetings Ralph went to the boss's hotel room to drive him to the track. While waiting for him to get ready he looked out the window and recognized several panhandlers standing in front of the entrance.

"I pointed them out to Mr. Kyne and told him I could

go down and get the car and meet him at the side entrance and we could duck them. He didn't say anything but felt in his pocket and then said, 'I don't have any money, do you?' I told him I had a twenty and he said, 'loan it to me until we get to the track.' I gave it to him and he got it changed at the desk and gave all the bums some quarters and halves."

This incident brings to mind another story about Kyne and panhandlers. In his earlier years there was a month or so when he was a daily customer at a San Francisco bookie joint. A group of moochers learned he would leave when the Eastern races were over and would be waiting for him for a handout. He never disappointed them—except for one day when he came out and said, "I'm sorry, fellows, I had a bad day and haven't got a dime in my pocket." Then he added with a smile, "But tomorrow you'll all get double."

But back to Cunningham. "We were at Del Mar and Bill gave me six hundred dollars and told me to bet it on a certain horse. I marked it on my program, got the tickets, and when I handed them to him he said, 'You got the wrong horse, lad.' I said no I didn't. I'd talk back to him when I knew I was right. It was too late to change them because the horses had just left the gate. The horse he had the tickets on won and paid a fair price. Don't remember how much he won, but it was a nice sum. But when I cashed the tickets and brought the money to him he was still irked."

On Kyne's sixty-ninth birthday, his last, Prescott Sullivan wrote in his column in the *San Francisco Examiner* on May 1, 1956:

. . . Bill Kyne doesn't look 69. Doesn't act it, either. The squire of Bay Meadows never had the time to grow old. With him were too many irons in the fire and too many big deals cooking to permit the cultivation of long, gray whiskers.

At an age that entitled him to take it easy, Kyne remains as restlessly active as he was when he was a kid of 13 hawking papers at the old Emeryville track. Since then he has been alternately broke and in the chips many times, but the marks of the rising and falling financial tides don't show. His belief that everything will turn out all right has kept a smile on his face through some mighty dark moments.

In his more than half a century in racing, Kyne has done about everything there is to do around a race track except ride in a race. Retirement has never entered his mind.

"I'll quit when I'm dead and not before," he says. "I couldn't stop, anyhow, even if I wanted to. Too many people who have been with me for years are dependent on me for their jobs and I'm not going to let them down . . . Things were never better for me or for Bay Meadows. Everything is turning out fine. I always knew it would."

But things weren't as fine as Kyne wanted to believe. For several years he had had cirrhosis of the liver, and as he grew older the condition gradually became worse. His doctors told him it was important that he dispense with all forms of alcohol, and for a while he did, but he had been a regular, though moderate, drinker since his youth, and breaking the habit was difficult. After a few weeks of no drinks he went back to his usual bottle of Heineken beer with lunch and a couple of Scotch highballs before dinner. One habit he did quit, though, was smoking. He had stopped smoking cigarettes in the early 1950s.

But as late as the fall of 1956 Bill Kyne was still being the promoter of extravaganza. He arranged for the importation of ten Thoroughbreds from Argentina to Bay Meadows. They arrived at San Francisco Airport in a converted Pan American airliner on September 14, and it was the first time a plane load of horses had been flown from a foreign country.

Earlier in the year Kyne had gone to South America on a vacation, and at Buenos Aires he met three breeders of Thoroughbreds—Alberto Sanchez Morteo, Pablo Spinelli, and Eduardo Carrera. Later he completed the deal for the trio to ship the horses, race them, and offer them for sale at Bay Meadows' fall meeting. Kyne put up seventeen thousand dollars expense money to be repaid from winnings and/or sales, if any. In addition to the publicity value of foreign horses racing at Bay Meadows, Kyne expected some of them to be used later for breeding and believed the foreign bloodlines would benefit the state's Thoroughbred breeding industry.

Some of Kyne's friends thought he was foolish to risk his money in such a deal, pointing out that he knew very little about the Argentine men and less about their horses, except for one, a stakes winner named Holandes. Kyne knew it was a gamble, but Kyne was a gambler and he figured this was a risk worth taking.

To show off the Argentine imports and to gain advance publicity, Kyne decided to have a coming-out party on the Sunday before opening of the race meeting and invite the press and some friends. Then Kyne got to thinking, and the more Kyne would think the bigger he would think. Why not, he thought, invite the public and serve free food and drinks? And that's what he did.

He announced the public was invited to an open house at Bay Meadows to see the new horses on parade and that the track would serve free fried chicken, hot dogs, hamburgers, beans, cole slaw, coffee and whisky, beer and soft drinks, plus entertainment. He personally invited members of the South American consulates.

"These are fine Thoroughbreds," Kyne proclaimed, "and they should be introduced to the American public in a style befitting their royal blood."

The ebullient squire of Bay Meadows prepared for a crowd of ten thousand, and it's a good thing he did, because a throng estimated at that number came to the track. The horses were paraded in front of the stands and several

Bill Kyne leading Holandes down ramp from plane after the horse's arrival from Argentina.

went through workouts. Announcer Hal Moore introduced them over the PA system. Entertainers from the Sinaloa nightclub sang and danced, and music was provided by Harry Mason's band, which used as its theme song, "The Best Things in Life Are Free."

It was probably the largest and most expensive party ever given by a racetrack.

The foreign horses proved worthy of the fanfare and publicity. Each won at least one race, and three, Holandes, Posadas, and Eugenio, went on to win stakes races.

Holandes, a three-year-old, was a stakes winner in Argentina and was rated one of South America's three best Thoroughbreds. Holandes won the Bay Meadows Handicap, with Eugenio second, and was purchased by Carl De Benedetti, Don Wood, and Bob Roberts for one hundred thousand dollars. The following spring Holandes missed winning the one hundred thousand dollar Santa Anita Handicap by a nose. De Benedetti also bought Eugenio for twenty-five thousand dollars. Posadas was sold to Anita King and Harry Brown for twenty-five thousand dollars.

By the end of the meeting all of the horses from Argentina had been sold and several were later retired to breeding farms.

The venture in importing the horses from South America had proved an outstanding success from all angles.

It was Kyne's last big promotion project.

The Argentine horses were crowd attracters, but so were some of America's top horses and jockeys who have competed at the track that Kyne built.

Seabiscuit began his climb to fame and fortune at the San Mateo course after being claimed by C. S. Howard for eight thousand dollars. Triple Crown winner Citation raced there, as did Kentucky Derby winners Determine and Majestic Prince, and Noor, Round Table, Native Diver, and many other ranking stakes horses.

Nationally known jockey stars who have ridden at Bay Meadows include Bill Shoemaker, Johnny Longden, Laffit Pincay, Jr., Manuel Ycaza, Johnny Adams, George Woolf, Jack Westrope, Jack (Red) Pollard, and Bill Hartack.

The 1956 race meeting was a record-breaker, and after it closed in mid-December the affable boss of Bay Meadows began preparing for the spring season to open February 22.

Then his health began to decline more rapidly. Shortly after Christmas he was confined to his home on doctor's orders and told to rest and take a nap each day. But Kyne made his home his office and began transacting business from there. His secretary would go in each day with mail and business matters from the track, and he worked on preparations for the next meeting.

In mid-January he spent a week in St. Francis Hospital for tests and treatment. Though he was a sick man, Kyne got a laugh from a telegram sent from Florida by a former jockey who had ridden at some of Kyne's tracks. It read:

Dear Friend Mr. Kyne:

I am sorry to learn that you are in the hospital and I hope you get well. One thing, though, you have made a success in racing where I have had it hard and still am. I wish you would leave me something in your will as I need a new start and if you fail to recover you can go to heaven having done a very good deed. You can't take it with you. Your sincere friend.

Lester Dye
Care Hialeah Race Track

When Kyne returned home his doctor still wouldn't permit him to go to his office at the track. Though he was ill physically, his mind was clear, alert, and active, and Mrs. Kyne had difficulty getting him to rest as the doctor ordered. Then on Tuesday, February 12, his condition became worse and his doctor put him back in the hospital.

Marylin recalls that his morale was still good at this point and his mind sharp. When I asked her if she thought Bill realized during the latter weeks of his illness that he might not recover, she replied, "Yes, I think he did, but to protect my mother from worrying he didn't want her to know, and he didn't seem depressed.

"Once, though, I heard my mother say, 'But what will I do without you?' and Dad said in a very kind voice, 'Don't worry, you will be all right. You have Marylin and your grandchildren and people who love you, and you'll be fine.'

"It was very hard on Mother. They had a very happy relationship. He got a lot out of life. He enjoyed living.

"Just before he went to the hospital he said to me: 'Always be kind and sweet—and pay your bills. And God be with you.'"

On the third day after he entered the hospital the second time, Bill Kyne lapsed into a coma. His physician, Dr. Emile D. Torre, stated:

"Everything known to medical science for his condition [liver ailment] is being done, but it is a losing battle." The doctor said Kyne was waging a determined battle, and added:

"A patient unconsciously can give way or fight. Mr. Kyne is giving it a fight."

In the *Examiner* of Friday, February 15, Sports Editor Curley Grieve wrote, in part, under the headline, "Wife Keeps Vigil As Hope Fades For Noted Turfman":

> Condition of William P. Kyne was unchanged late last night and little hope was held that he could win his fight for life.
>
> The executive director of Bay Meadows, one of the last of the great individual promoters, was in a coma at St. Francis Hospital. His wife, Dorothy, and daughter, Mrs. Robert Gunderson, were at his bedside.
>
> Kyne's closest friends and business associates had been alerted to expect the worst within 24 hours.

But despite this sad news Bill's helpers at Bay Meadows went ahead with plans for the track's opening next week.

Kyne, 69, who has been ill for several weeks and re-entered the hospital only last Tuesday, had looked ahead toward the coming meeting with great expectations. He had felt that perhaps it might be his last and he wanted it to be his best. . . .

Bill had not forgotten an important function during the last week. He had prepared his personal pass list so all his friends would be able to get into the track without cost. He personally had gone over the long list of names with his secretary, Mrs. Mae De Vol, who visited him daily.

Kyne, from home and hospital, had directed such track improvements as grading of roads in the barn area, painting of barns, installing a new drainage system in the barn area and construction of an aluminum goose-neck inner rail on the racing strip. The club house betting area also was glass-enclosed and the grandstand refurbished. . . .

The following morning, Saturday, February 16, Kyne's wife, daughter, and brothers Jack and Tom were at his bedside, and at 10:15 his heart stopped beating.

Surviving the colorful sportsman in addition to his wife and daughter, sister, and two brothers were three grandchildren. The ages of the grandchildren at that time were Gretchen, nine; Greg, six; and Nancy, nine months. Another grandchild, Grant, was born later.

All of the Bay Area newspapers carried lengthy stories on Bill Kyne's funeral, and the story by Prescott Sullivan in the *San Francisco Examiner* won the local Press Club's award as the year's best story by a sports writer. Here is Sullivan's story:

Wrapped in the familiar gray robe in which many of her children think she looks her best, San Francisco yesterday said farewell to a favorite son.

The fog shrouded goodbye was for William Patrick "Bill" Kyne, who was laid to rest in Golden Gate National Cemetery just across the highway from Tanforan race track in which he once had an interest.

The colorful 69 year old race track figure passed away last Saturday. Death followed a long illness but almost until the last Kyne had worked on plans for the opening of the Bay Meadows meeting this Friday.

Hundreds of mourners joined in paying him their last respects. At Halsted's they filled the chapel to overflowing and at the cemetery they stood in moist eyed silence as the moving graveside rites were performed and the cooling mist, which had caressed his cheeks so many times in life, swirled around the beloved "Squire of Bay Meadows" for the last time.

Black-jacketed professionals, some weeping a little because they too remembered Kyne as a friend, said it was the "biggest funeral in years." The cortege, which reached Kyne's last resting place, by way of California St., 19th Ave., and Junipero Serra Blvd., was blocks long.

Pallbearers were Joe Cohen, Harold Mundhenk, Eddie Benn and Bob McNeil, long time associates at Bay Meadows; two nephews, John and William E. Kyne; William Uniack, the son of Kyne's old pal, the late Al Uniack, and Carl De Benedetti, San Mateo contractor and horseman.

To All Men He Was A Friend

The mourners, proof of the universal appeal of Kyne's warm-hearted personality, represented all walks of life. Among them were financiers, business leaders, politicians, race track officials, policemen, gamblers, clergymen and swipes. All had known Kyne's kindly touch and all were in common cause. To each and every one, Kyne was a friend.

Ex-police chiefs Charlie Dullea and Mike Mitchell; Slip Madigan, the old football Coach; Tote Naveside, the tug and barge man; Webb Everett of Golden Gate Fields; Fred Ryan of Tanforan; big Walter Schulken; little Richie Roberts; former sports editors Pat Frayne and Tom Laird; Dave Butler, the movie director, and Tom Maloney, the assemblyman, who helped Kyne in his fight to restore horse racing in California, were just a few of the hundreds who filed past Kyne's bier.

Mayor George Christopher was on hand. So were Dwight Murphy, chairman of the Racing Commission; Bill Gilmore, the steel tycoon; Ernie Nevers, the old football star, and Willie Kamm, baseball's "$100,000 beauty" of 35 years ago.

Down from Reno was Bill Graham, the gambler. Up from

Santa Anita was Bert Thompson, of the Jockeys Guild, and in from Denver was Ivan Thomas, one of a good many men now prominent in racing who owe their starts to Kyne.

In the heterogeneous demonstration of the esteem in which Kyne was held by his fellow San Franciscans, bankers rubbed elbows with touts and aged madams, grotesquely rouged and painted reminders of the gay past, bowed their heads along with fine ladies from Nob Hill.

The Chapel Was Too Small

The chapel at Halsted's wasn't nearly big enough to hold them all. Kyne, always the expansive promoter, might have foreseen that and made a joke of it by saying "next time we get the Cow Palace."

At the cemetery, the services were brief. Rev. Father John O'Brien of Mill Valley said a prayer for the deceased. A military honor guard fired a three gun salute. An Army bugler played taps and six soldiers carefully removed and folded the American flag from the casket.

The flag was replaced by a spray of roses and presented to Kyne's widow, Dorothy, who sat at graveside in the company of other members of the family. Then each of the eight pallbearers placed a white carnation on top of the steel-grey coffin and the mourners slowly dispersed, leaving others to lower Kyne's mortal remains into the ground.

Father O'Brien wept as he walked away. To his prayers he added an unclerical expression of the depth of his feelings.

"This was a great guy," he said softly.

The same words or their equivalent meaning were on every lip. Les Vogel, Jr., the automobile tycoon, repeated them. So did Shanty Malone, Willie Ritchie, Joe "The Toe" Vetrano, Sheriff Earl Whitmore of San Mateo County and Joe "Waffle Ear" Malcewicz, the wrestling promoter.

They were heard from millionaires and mendicants, bartenders and barristers; bookmakers and cops; doctors, bus drivers, stable hands, judges—as on a foggy morning so characteristic of the city of his birth, a great guy went to his last resting place.

In life Bill Kyne had taken the many doses of bitter that fate had meted out to him. Now he had gone where there would be no more bitter—only the sweet.

20

The death of Bill Kyne occurred six days before Bay Meadows was scheduled to open on February 22, and appointment of a general manager was a matter of expediency. On February 19 the board of directors elected Bill's widow as his successor. Mrs. Kyne was considered a logical choice because of her close association with Bill's work, and was therefore familiar with his operation of the track. Joe Cohen was elected vice-president and named director of racing, and Bill Hornblower retained his position as president.

Dorothy Kyne proved a capable manager, but replacing Bill Kyne was not an easy task, and sitting at the desk he had occupied so many years brought back memories. It was difficult for her to enjoy the work, and after two seasons she resigned.

Joe Cohen succeeded her and served as general manager and president from 1959 to 1969, when he resigned at the age of seventy-four.

The directors had no difficulty filling the vacancy. They appointed Bob Gunderson.

Gunderson at that time was general manager of Tanforan and Golden Gate Fields, in addition to being assistant manager and vice-president at Bay Meadows. He resigned

After becoming general manager, Dorothy Kyne gave a press party at Roberts-At-The Beach. She is shown here with several of her guests: (left to right) Curley Grieve, Examiner *sports editor; Jack McDonald,* Call-Bulletin *sports editor; Prescott Sullivan,* Examiner *columnist, and Will Connolly,* Chronicle *columnist.*

the former positions to devote full time to the track that Kyne built. Les Vogel, Jr., succeeded Cohen as president. In 1973 Vogel was elected chairman of the board, and Gunderson became president.

The appointment of Gunderson to the top management job would have pleased Bill Kyne. He had expected his son-in-law to succeed him, and actually Bob could have had the job when Kyne died, but he declined because he thought it might look as though he were getting the position through nepotism. He wanted the position, but he wanted to gain it on his own.

Officers and directors of the William P. Kyne Memorial Thoroughbred Library: Front row, from left, Cecilia DeMille Harper, president; Gretchen Kramer, librarian; Lillian B. Dwyer; Grace Knoop, secretary; Kent Cochran, vice-president. Back row, Bob Wuerth; Dr. William J. Ward; Herb Phipps; Barry Whitehead, treasurer; George G. Gaugler.

When Gunderson did take over the peninsula track he followed the Kyne policy of emphasis on progress and promotion. During the nine years he has been at the helm he has made vast improvements throughout the plant, and outstanding among his promotional projects are establishment of the one hundred thousand dollar El Camino Real Stakes, one of the jewels in the Western Triple Crown for juveniles, and the annual Bay Meadows Ascot Day. The Ascot Day is a popular and colorful event patterned after the Ascot Gold Cup festivities at the famous old track at Berkshire, England.

166

Among improvements are the infield turf course, an underground tunnel to new facilities in the infield for spectators, and the glass enclosure of the Turf Club.

In 1974 Gunderson built new administration offices and a large room for the William P. Kyne Memorial Thoroughbred Library, first proposed by his daughter Gretchen.

In his address dedicating the library, Les Vogel said: "This fine library is a fitting tribute to the man whose foresight and determined efforts against huge odds brought about the return of horse racing to California forty years ago. The William P. Kyne Memorial Library fulfills a need in Northern California and at the same time honors a deserving and fondly remembered man."

If Bill Kyne could return for a brief visit to Bay Meadows he probably would make an inspection tour, then express his approval with a smile and comment, "Well done."

Index

Adams, Johnny, 28, 159
Agajanian, J. C., 111
Agua Caliente, 16, 122
Agua Caliente Cup, 122
Anderson, Bronco Billy, 12, 14
Aqueduct, 16
Arnaz, Desi, 90
Ascot Day at Bay Meadows, 97, 160
Attell, Abe, 11

Baer, Max, 19
Baldwin, Lucky, 40
Barlow, Ed, 65, 68
Barnes, Ralph, 136, 138
Battson, Leigh, 40
Bay Meadows Handicap, 46, 158
Beckwith, B. K., 6
Beebe, Tom, 46
Beery, Wallace, 12, 13, 14
Belmont Park, 145
Benn, Eddie, 53, 62, 66, 162
Blackie, 73, 74, 76
Blair, Don, 58
Bondy's, 53
Brennan, Michael, 143, 145
Britt, Jimmy, 11
Brooks, Steve, 91
Brown, Edmund G. (Pat), 146
Brown, Harry, 158

Browning, Edward (Daddy), 132, 133
Browning, Peaches, 132
Brundage, Rusty, 6, 122
Buck, C. A., 42
Burke, Carleton F., 37, 39
Busky, George, 102, 103, 104, 105, 106, 148
Butler, Dave, 162

California Horse Racing Association, 15
California Horse Racing Board, 37, 42, 143
California Jockey Club, 37, 39, 43, 62
Calumet Stable, 91
Cantu, Governor Esteban, 15
Carraud, Frank, 46
Carrera, Eduardo, 156
Carrington, Walter, 122
Carter, Jimmy, 146
Cassidy, Marshall, 120
Champion, Hale, 146, 147
Chaplin, Charlie, 13
Chapultepec, 121
Charles, Ezzard, 109
Chevalier, Maurice, 89, 90
Choctaw, The, 122

Christopher, Mayor George, 162
Churchill Downs, 28
Church, Norman W., 32, 34
Citation, 91, 158
Clayton, Ethel, 12
Cobb, Ty, 62, 63
Cochran, Kent, 166
Coffroth, James (Sunny Jim), 14, 16
Cohen, Joe, 72, 77, 126, 134, 136, 137, 162, 164
Cole, Nat King, 90
College of Notre Dame, 89, 128
Comstock, Harry, 38
Conners, Chuck, 90
Connolly, Will, 6, 149, 165
Copeland, Bruce, 106, 107
Corbett, Gentleman Jim, 107
Corn Husker, 81
Cotton, Mayor A. R., 42, 43
Crosby, Bing, 122, 129
Cunningham, Ralph, 6, 58, 70, 153, 154
Curran, Mickey, 67, 68

Dailey, Dan, 90
Davidson, Johnny, 150
Davis, D. J., 58
De Benedetti, Carl, 6, 80, 158, 162
Del Mar, 60, 151, 154
Dempsey, Jack, 19, 20, 38
Determine, 158
De Vol, Frank, 6
De Vol, Mae Feist, 5, 49, 124, 125, 136, 161
De Vol, Steve, 6
De Witt, Lt. Gen. John J., 82
Diamond, Jimmy, 11
Dougherty, Charlie, 6, 123, 124
Doyle, Bobby, 123
Dressler, Marie, 12
Dullea, Charlie, 162
Duncan Sisters, 90, 91, 143, 144, 145
Dwyer Handicap, 16
Dwyer, Lillian B., 166

Dwyer, Mickey, 6, 20, 28, 41
Dye, Lester, 159

El Camino Real Stakes, 166
Elliott, Vi, 109
El Lobo, 117
Emeryville Race Track, 9
Essanay Studio, 12
Eugenio, 158
Everett, Webb, 162

Faisal, Prince, 128, 129
Falk, Lew, 26
Featherfoot, 117
Finn, The, 121
Fitzsimmons, Bob, 107
Flynn, Frank, 79
Flynn, Tom, 52
Frayne, Pat, 162

Gaugler, George G., 166
Gerken, Grace, 6, 152, 153
Gilmore, Ben, 124
Gilmore, Bill, 162
Gleason, Jimmy, 12
Goglin, A. J., 138
Golden Gate Fields, 93, 164
Grable, Betty, 111
Graham, Bill, 162
Granny, 138, 141
Great Train Robbery, The, 12
Greenback, Bill, 80
Greenslade, Admiral, 153
Greive, Curley, 134, 160, 165
Gresham race meetings, 19, 41
Gunderson, Grant, 161
Gunderson, Greg, 97, 161
Gunderson, Gretchen, 161. See also Kramer, Gretchen Gunderson
Gunderson, Marylin Kyne, 5, 56, 58, 93, 94, 96, 123, 160, 164, 166, 167
Gunderson, Nancy, 97, 161
Gunderson, Robert S. (Bob), 5, 93, 94, 96, 123, 164, 165, 166, 167

170

Gymkhana Club, 45

Hackett, Ray, 111
Halsey, Admiral, 153
Hamblen, Stuart, 117, 118
Harbormaster, 139, 147
Harper, Cecilie DeMille, 166
Hartack, Bill, 159
Hearst, William Randolph, 32, 36, 39
Henry O., 153
Hernandez, Joe, 119
Hoelle, Major Bill, 117
Hoertkorn, Harold, 6
Holandes, 81, 156, 157, 158
Hooker, Robert G., 42
Hornblower, William B. (Bill), 35, 36, 51, 52, 134
Howard, Anita, 129
Howard, Charles S., 129, 158
Howard, Lin, 129
Hughes, Howard, 91
Hunter, Charlie, 123, 124
Hunt, Thomas, 42

Iglesias, Rafeal, 109
Ironmen's Social Club, 12

James, Harry, 111
Jarvis, Jack, 120, 121
Jeffers, William M., 82
Jeffrey, Jim, 107
Jim Dandy, 10
John Graham, 14
John P. Grier, 17
Johnson, Jack, 12
Jones, Ben, 28
Jones, Jimmy, 91
J. O. Tobin, 28
Juarez race meetings, 10, 22
Jurgens, Dick, 111

Kamm, Willie, 162
Kansas City race meetings, 20, 27, 63, 64, 65

Kearns, Jack, 38
Kemp, Abe, 46, 150
Kentucky Derby, 158
Kerr, Myrtle, 55
Khalid, Prince, 128, 129
Killian, Eddie, 27
King, Admiral, 153
King, Anita, 158
King's Currency, 138
King, Walter, 23
Knoop, Grace, 166
Kramer, Gretchen Gunderson, 5, 166
Kyne, Dorothy, 13, 44, 59, 133, 159, 160, 164, 165
Kyne, Ellen, 10
Kyne, George, 10
Kyne, Grace, 10
Kyne, Jack, 10, 11, 161, 162
Kyne, John, 10, 11
Kyne, Marylin. See Gunderson, Marylin
Kyne, Nelle. See Morris, Nelle Kyne
Kyne, Peter B., 43
Kyne, Rose, 10
Kyne, Tom, 10, 161
Kyne, William K. (Willie), 5, 20, 41, 121, 162

La Barba, Fidel, 90
Laird, Tom, 46, 162
Leighninger, R. E. (Lanny), 6, 101, 117
Lemon, Bob, 90
Longden, Johnny, 19, 159
Los Angeles Turf Club, 40
Louis, Joe, 90, 109
Lower California Jockey Club, 15, 16

McCarthy, Clem, 119
McCrory, Phil, 27
McDaniel, R. H., 75
McDonald, Jack, 46, 165
McGonigle, 121, 122

McNaughton, John A., 37
McNeil, Bob, 162
McQueen, George, 148
McQueen, Gloria, 148
Madigan, Slip, 162
Majestic Prince, 158
Malcewicz, Joe, 163
Malone, Shanty, 163
Malone, Tom, 11, 35, 36, 52, 162
Manners, Man, 129, 130
Man o' War, 16, 17
Marchbank, John W., 23, 26, 32, 39
Marchison, Doug, 6
Mare Island Naval Hospital, 85, 89
Marshall, George, 134, 135
Mason, Harry, 158
Mathieson, Rusty, 5, 132
Mayer, Louis B., 129, 130, 131
Meehan, Lawler, 14, 17
Menges, Jack, 135
Mighty Regal, 138
Miss Fashion Plate, 24
Mitchell, Mike, 162
Molly O, 81
Monteux, Pierre, 128, 130
Moore, Hal, 158
Moran, Willie, 122
Morris, Nelle Kyne, 5, 10, 13, 18
Morrison, H. M. (Sec), 20, 63, 64, 65
Morteo, Alberto Sanchez, 155
Moyle, Dorothy, 55
Mundhenk, Harold, 80, 162
Murfee, Emerson, 54
Murphy, Dwight, 162
Murphy, George, 21, 22, 55, 143, 144, 145
Murphy, J. J., 46, 119
Murphy, Joseph A., 23
Murray, Jimmy, 109

Naify, Mike, 80
Native Diver, 158
Naveside, Tote, 162
Necessary, 139, 140

Nevers, Ernie, 162
Neves, Ralph, 141
New York Giants, 112
Nimitz, Admiral, 153
Noor, 158
Nordoff, Diane, 6
Normile, Gene, 38, 77

O'Brien, Father John, 163
O'Doul, Frank (Lefty), 77
O'Farrell, Tom, 69
Olson, Bobo, 109
Olson, Governor Culbert, 37
O'Neill, John, 6, 38
Osterhaus, Admiral, 153
Otis, Oscar, 24, 26, 46
Owen, Lee, 46

Pacific Coast Breeders' Association, 32, 34
Pacific Coast Trotting Association, 115
Panerio, George, 80
Patterson, Mel, 5
Paul, C. C., 64
Pendergast, T. J., 6, 27
Peninsula Horse Racing Association, 115
Phar Lap, 58
Phoenix race meetings, 19, 20
Pierce, June, 6, 152
Pincay, Lafitt, Jr., 159
Pitts, Zasu, 12
Pollard, Jack (Red), 159
Pomeroy, Walter, 75
Portland Meadows, 93, 122, 123, 124, 126, 151, 153
Posadas, 158
Puett, Clay, 119, 120, 121

Rapid Bell, 46
Redneck, 121
Reno race meetings, 19
Richardson Springs, 29
Ritchie, Willie, 11, 163

172

Riverside Park, 27, 28
Roach, Hal, 38, 40
Roberts-At-The-Beach, 53, 73, 75
Roberts, Bob, 158
Robertson, Bill, 6
Robertson, Dale, 90
Roberts, Richie (Shorty), 73, 76, 162
Roberts, Wilford, 73
Robinson, Sugar Ray, 109
Rockne, Knute, 80
Rockingham Park, 38
Rolph, Governor James, 36
Romero, Ed, 6, 135
Rooney, Mickey, 69, 90
Rose, George, 14
Roth, William P., 37, 42
Round Table, 158
Ruben, Alma, 13
Runyon, Damon, 69
Ryan, Fred, 162

Sagehorn, A. H., 42
St. Anthony's Dining Room, 18
St. Francis Hospital, 159, 160
St. Francis Jockey Club, 38
St. Patrick's Church, 9
Salt Lake City Race Track, 56
Samish, Artie, 78
San Francisco Children's Hospital Auxiliary, 101
San Francisco Seals, 38
San Joaquin County Fair, 41
San Jose Handicap, 135
San Mateo County Fair Association, 115
Santa Anita Handicap, 81
Santa Anita Park, 41, 47, 128
Saratoga, 10
Schilling, George, 71, 117, 118, 119, 151
Schrieber, Barney, 12, 14
Schulken, Walter, 162
Seabiscuit, 129, 158
Sharkey, Tom, 101

Shoemaker, Bill, 158
Silver State Jockey Club, 19
Sims, Charlie, 143
Slavin, Patrick (Duck In), 71, 72
Smith, Harry B., 26
Smith, Jack, 6, 87, 88, 89
Smith, Lou, 38
Smoot, Joe, 38
Sonny Marcus, 121
Soule, Ed, 14
Sparks, Art, 28, 41
Spinelli, Pablo, 155
Stanford, Leland, 43
Strub, Dr. Charles H., 38, 39, 40, 42
Strub, Robert P. (Bob), 46
Sullivan, Captain Bob, 117
Sullivan, Neil (Dirty Shirt), 70
Sullivan, Prescott, 6, 83, 154, 161, 165
Swig, Ben, 131

Tanforan, 23, 25, 26, 31, 39, 41, 93
Tatum, Burl, 117, 118
Thomas, Ivan, 123, 163
Thompson, Bert, 163
Thornton, Edward, 28
Thoroughbred Racing Associations, 46
Tichner, Solly, 18, 64, 75, 77, 133
Time Supply, 46
Torre, Dr. Emile D., 160
Torres, Al, 111
Travres Stakes, 10
Travis Air Base Hospital, 90
Truman, Harry S., 27
Tucker, Sophie, 73
Tulsa race meetings, 19, 23
Turpin, Ben, 12

Uncle Tom's Cabin, 53
Uniack, Al, 11, 32, 37, 40, 162
Uniack, William, 162
Union Athletic Club, 12
Universal Totalizator Company, 126

173

Uzcundun, Paulino, 19

Valentine, Pat, 109
Vessels, Frank, Sr., 113
Vetrano, Joe, 163
Villa Chartier, 53
Villa, Panco, 133, 134
Vogel, Les, Jr., 6, 80, 163, 165, 167

Walgast, Ad, 11
Walker, Andy, 109
Walker, Mickey, 90
Ward, Dr. William J., 6, 114, 115, 166
Warren, Earl, 78
Washington, George, 113
Welk, Lawrence, 90
Westrope, Jack, 159

Whitehead, Barry, 6, 166
Whitmore, Sheriff Earl, 163
Whittingham, Charlie, 25
Whittingham, Joe, 25
William K., 148, 149, 150
William P. Kyne Memorial Thoroughbred Library, 167
Wolfe, Dale, 141
Wood, Don, 158
Woolf, George, 159
Woolwine, Clare, 35
Wright, John (Geronimo), 69
Wuerth, Bob, 6, 69, 166

Yazzolino, Vi Elliott, 6, 109
Ycaza, Manuel, 159

Zarelli, George, 6, 151, 152